The *Collectio canonum Casinensis duodecimi saeculi (codex terscriptus)*

edited by
Roger E. Reynolds

This volume is a study and 'implicit' edition of a twelfth-century collection of ecclesiastical law made in the ancient home of the Benedictine order, Montecassino. The importance of the collection is fourfold: (1) it is the last canonical collection written in the Beneventan script, the beautiful and distinctive script used in southern Italy and Dalmatia from the late eighth to the late sixteenth century; (2) it is a significant canonical collection deriving from the important early eleventh-century canonical *Collection in Five Books*, a collection compiled probably at Montecassino that spawned at least twenty-five derivative collections from the late eleventh to the late twelfth centuries in southern and central Italy; (3) its canons reflect both early eleventh-century reforming trends of the Ottonian and Salian emperors and later eleventh-century reforming trends associated with the so-called Gregorian reformers; and (4) it contains a number of canons applicable to Montecassino itself, several of which are known only from this manuscript. Moreover, the manuscript in which the collection is found is interesting codicologically because two texts written beneath the current text have been erased or palimpsested to provide material for the canonical collection.

Since many of the texts found in the collection have been published elsewhere, the suggestion of the late Professor J. Joseph Ryan has been followed that an 'implicit' edition be made giving only the incipit or beginning and the explicit or end of each canon, together with an identification of the source of the canon and where a published or manuscript version of the canon may be found. Indices of incipits and attributions of the canons in the collection, as well as a subject index, conclude the volume.

Monumenta Liturgica Beneventana
III

Studies and Texts 137

The Collectio canonum Casinensis duodecimi seculi (Codex terscriptus)

A Derivative of the South-Italian
Collection in Five Books

An Implicit Edition with Introductory Study

by

Roger E. Reynolds

Pontifical Institute of Mediaeval Studies

This book has been published with the help of a grant
from the Humanities and Social Sciences Federation of Canada,
using funds provided by the Social Sciences and
Humanities Research Council of Canada.

CANADIAN CATALOGUING IN PUBLICATION DATA

Collectio canonum Casinensis
The Collectio canonum Casinensis duodecimi seculi (Codex terscriptus) : a derivative of the South-Italian Collection in five books : an implicit edition with introductory study

(Monumenta liturgica Beneventana ; 3)
(Studies and texts, ISSN 0082-5328 ; 137)
Text in Latin; introduction and notes in English.
Includes index.
ISBN 0-88844-137-1

1. Canon law – Early works to 1800. I. Reynolds, Roger E., 1936- . II. Montecassino (Monastery). III. Pontifical Institute of Mediaeval Studies. IV. Series. V. Series: Studies and texts (Pontifical Institute of Mediaeval Studies) ; 137.

K3282.C2C64 2001 262.909021 C00-932929-3

Pontifical Institute of Mediaeval Studies
59 Queen's Park Crescent East
Toronto, Ontario, Canada M5S 2C4

www.pims.ca

Manufactured in Canada

Contents

Preface vii

Introduction 1
Codicological and Palaeographical Description 10
Comments on Editorial Principles 15
Addenda 19

COLLECTIO CANONUM CASINENSIS
DUODECIM SAECULI

Edition with notes 33

Incipits 111
Attributions of Canons 122
Subject Index 126

Preface

In 1958 at the first international Congress of Medieval Canon Law held in Louvain and Brussels Msgr. J. J. Ryan of the Pontifical Institute of Mediaeval Studies in Toronto presented an overview of work being done at that time in the edition and study of pre-Gratian canonical collections. One of the collections he singled out was the early eleventh-century Italian *Collection in Five Books,* which shortly before had been partially edited and studied by Mario Fornasari in his thesis at the Lateran University in Rome. Some twelve years later Fornasari would produce an edition of Books I-III of the collection in the series *Corpus christianorum, Continuatio Mediaevalis.* This edition was a useful one, especially for its identification of the sources of the collection, but the edition was so severely criticized by reviewers that Fornasari's planned edition of Books IV-V never materialized.

It was Fornasari's contention that the *Collection in Five Books* had been compiled in Farfa, and hence as his base manuscript he used the codex, Vatican, BAV, Vat. lat. 1339, whose origins he located in Farfa. This manuscript, conveniently located in the Vatican Library, is written in the easy-to-read Romanesca script, not the Beneventan script of the one at Montecassino, MS 125. Since the time of Fornasari's publications it has become increasingly clear that the collection itself was compiled in southern Italy, eventually to be copied in manuscripts from Farfa or Narni and Sant'Eutizio presso Norcia. Further, it is evident that the manuscript likely written at Montecassino in Beneventan script should have been used as the base text because it is generally fuller than either of the other two more-or-less complete codices of the collection..

But whatever the origins of the *Collection in Five Books*, an edition of at least Books IV-V (if not the complete collection) remains a desideratum, not because the collection is found in multiple manuscripts of such collections as Burchard's *Decretum,* but because texts from the *Collection in Five Books* were used in multiple south and central

Italian collections, even beyond the time of Gratian. Many of these derivative collections – numbering almost twenty-five – contain texts whose contents would have been appropriate to the *Collection in Five Books* itself, and one suspects that in now lost manuscripts of the collection these texts were present. Hence, for a complete picture of the texts of the collection one would hope ideally that all of these collections could be studied and edited together with the *Collection in Five Books*. This ideal, however, is probably not possible unless an equipe of researchers were involved. Thus, a step in producing this ideal can be initiated by publishing editions and studies of the derivative and related collections, while awaiting a complete edition and study of the more extensive *Collection in Five Books*.

A question posed by Msgr. Ryan in 1958 then arises. Is it necessary to produce complete editions of these derivative and related collections that usually appear in a single manuscript and whose canons are frequently found in hitherto published collections? Here, Msgr. Ryan suggested that complete editions of collections be made only for what might be called 'key collections,' such as the late ninth-century *Collectio Anselmo dedicata* or the late eleventh-century *Collection in 74 Titles*. Probably he would also have considered the *Collection in Five Books* a 'key collection' for its size and wide influence. For other collections that are based on those already edited or in print, Msgr. Ryan suggested that 'implicit editions' be made containing: (1) rubrics (*tituli, capitulationes*) if any; (2) the inscription or citation of source; (3) the number of the *capitulum* as given in the collection, if any; (4) the *incipit* and *desinit* of the text; and 5) wherever possible, the source collection or *fons materialis* from which the text came.

Following this model, a beginning has been made in producing 'implicit' or incipit-explicit editions of some of the collections deriving from the *Collection in Five Books*. Two of these have appeared and more are planned: R. Reynolds, 'The South-Italian *Collection in Five Books* and its Derivatives: the *Collection of Vallicelliana Tome XXI*,' *Proceedings of the Eighth International Congress of Medieval Canon Law: San Diego, University of California at La Jolla, 21-27 August 1988*, ed. S. Chodorow, Monumenta Iuris Canonici, Ser. C, Subsidia 9 (Vatican, 1991) 77-92; and 'The South Italian *Collection in Five Books* and Its Derivatives: Maastricht Excerpta,' Miscellanea Beneventana: Juridica, *Mediaeval Studies* 58 (1996) 273-28. It is hoped that another of the derivative collections, the *Collectio Toletana* edited by Dr. Douglas Adamson in his licentiate thesis at the Pontifical Institute of Mediaeval Studies in 1987 will soon supplement these. The publication here of an 'implicit edition' of the *Collectio canonum Casinensis*, the 'youngest' derivative of the *Collection in Five Books*, can be seen as part of this series, and its appearance as a volume in the Monumenta Liturgica Beneventana is appropriate in view of the number of liturgical canons in the collection and the Beneventan script in which the collection is written.

In presenting this 'implicit edition' one is aware that while many of the canons can be found in hitherto printed or edited collections –Burchard's *Decretum* and the *Collection in 74 Titles*, for example– one can cite from a printed text of the *Collection in Five Books* itself only those canons from Books I-III edited by Fornasari. Hence, one must cite manuscript sources for canons taken from Books IV-V. This has been done here with the hope that in the near future an edition of Books IV-V (either in a complete or 'implicit' edition) will appear to simplify matters for users of these derivative collections.

Research for this study has been generously supported by the Social Sciences and Humanities Research Council of Canada for the program Monumenta Liturgica Beneventana. For their kindness, assistance, and friendship along the way as research for and writing of this volume was done I owe a heavy debt of gratitude, both to non-medievalists and professional medievalists alike: Leda and Vittorio D'Errico, Lidia and Fernando Miele, Etienne and Marlene Odekerken, Robert Somerville, Uta-Renate Blumenthal, Charles Hilken, Richard F. Gyug, Mimi Gyug, Lioubov Ivanitskaia, Noel McCain, Virginia Brown, James Hankins, Jonathan Black, Don Mariano Dell'Omo, O.S.B., and Don Faustino Avagliano, O.S.B.

Pontifical Institute of Mediaeval Studies

Introduction

It has been conventional textbook wisdom that after the anarchy, corruption, and mismanagement of the Church in the post-Carolingian period of the late ninth and tenth centuries, measures to renew the Church were first introduced by the so-called Gregorian reformers in the second half of the eleventh century. Over the past half century this textbook wisdom has given way to a recognition that the Church was undergoing reform long before 1050.[1] On the one hand, it is now emphasized that from the time of the emperor Saint Henry II there was a genuine concern for the health and purity of the Church and that despite and, indeed, because of their heavy control of the Church, Henry and then the Salians installed a number of bishops, abbots, and even popes with these same concerns. On the canon law side, Henry II even 'legislated' on ecclesiastical matters in canons containing anathemas, something usually reserved to ecclesiastical legislation.[2] Further, it has been demonstrated that long before the mid-eleventh century, collections of canons looking toward reform of morals in the Church were being compiled and widely distributed which, although not emphasizing papal prerogatives, were nonetheless aimed at regularizing and purifying the life of the Church. Pride of place among these early eleventh-century collections has always gone to the *Decretum* of Burchard of Worms, widely disseminated north of the Alps and now known to have been in Italian libraries by the 1030s.[3] In fact, J. J. Ryan demonstrated that

[1] I owe this valuable observation to Giles Constable, from whom I first learned it in his introductory course in medieval history at Harvard. It was pointed out there that historians usually emphasize the ecclesiastical reforms of the Carolingian and Gregorian ages, but aside from monastic reforms, they generally do not dwell on reforms of the Church at large attempted between those two periods.

[2] See below, canon CCLXXXIII.

[3] See Nonantola, San Silvestro (three manuscripts numbered 11, 142, 151; cf. inventory anno post 1035; invent. anno 1331: no. 40; cf. J. Ruysschaert, *Les manuscrits de l'Abbaye de Nonantola. Table de concordance annotée et index des man-*

the reform-minded Peter Damian was most heavily influenced in his writings by the *Decretum*, which has traditionally been contrasted with the collections compiled and used by the reformers.[4]

In Italy itself from the beginning of the eleventh century canonical collections were being compiled, and although they differed from the *Decretum* of Burchard in their organization and texts used, they nevertheless played a parallel role in the reform of the Church in Italy, particularly the central and southern parts of the peninsula. Chief among these collections was one compiled in the south of Italy, the *Collection in Five Books*. This canonical collection dates probably to sometime in the 1020s.[5] It exists in only three manuscripts and one fragment.[6] But its influence on subsequent collections was significant well into the twelfth century, [7] despite the fact that the great

---

uscrits, Studi e testi 182bis [Vatican, 1955] p. 38).

[4] J. J. Ryan, *Saint Peter Damiani and his Canonical Sources. A Preliminary Study in the Antecedents of the Gregorian Reform*, Studies and Texts 2 (Toronto, 1956). The popularity of Burchard's *Decretum* can be seen in the great number of manuscripts known to have been or that are still extant (beyond the *Corrector* or L. XIX which also had an independent transmission as a type of penitential); see below, Addendum A, p. 19.

[5] R. Reynolds, 'The South-Italian Canon Law *Collection in Five Books* and its derivatives: new evidence on its origins, diffusion and use,' *Mediaeval Studies* 52 (1990) pp. 278-295; and 'South and Central Italian Canonical Collections of the Tenth and Eleventh Centuries (non-Gregorian),' *Studies in Medieval and Early Medieval Canon Law*, eds. W. Hartmann and K. Pennington (Washington, D. C., in press since 1993).

[6] Montecassino, Archivio dell'Abbazia, 125 (saec. XI^{med}; Montecassino); Roma, Biblioteca Vallicelliana, B 11 (saec. XI, before 1087); Sant' Eutizio in Val Castoriana, near Norcia); and R 32 (fol.50) (saec. XI$^{3/4}$; middle Italy) [fragment?]; Vaticano, Città del, Biblioteca Apostolica Vaticana, Vat. lat. 1339 (saec. XI^{med}; Italy, provenance Santa Maria, Narni).

[7] See P. Fournier, 'Un groupe de recueils canoniques italiens des Xe et XIe siècles,' *Mémoires de l'Institut National de France de l'Académie des Inscriptions et Belles-Lettres* 40 (Paris, 1916) pp. 95-213; repr. in *P. Fournier, Mélanges de droit canonique*, ed. T. Kölzer (Aalen, 1983) 2, pp. 213-331; P. Fournier, 'De l'influence de la collection irlandaise sur la formation des collections canoniques,' *Nouvelle revue historique de droit français et étranger* 23 (1899) pp. 27-78; repr. in *Mélanges de droit canonique* 2, pp. 93-144; P. Fournier and G. Le Bras, *Histoire des collections canoniques en Occident depuis les Fausses Décrétales jusqu'au Décret de Gratien* (Paris, 1931-32: repr. Aalen, 1972) 1, pp. 421-431; T. Kölzer, (ed.), *Collectio canonum Regesto Farfensi inserta*, Monumenta Iuris Canonici, Series B: Corpus Collectionum 5 (Vatican City, 1982) pp. 48-55 (§§42-46); R. Reynolds, 'A South Italian ordin-

collections connected with the reform of the church in the latter half of the eleventh century–the *Collection in 74 Titles*,[8] the *Collectio canonum* of Anselm of Lucca,[9] and the northern collections of Ivo of Chartres, his *Tripartita*,[10] *Decretum*,[11]and *Panormia*[12]–came to dominate among canonistic compilations used throughout Europe, a fact clearly seen in their extensive manuscript diffusions.

There were several reasons for the continuing influence of the south-Italian *Collection in Five Books*. First, it contained many useful canons from the patristic fathers and penitentials that other collections lacked. Second, its canons were combined very quickly in many derivative collections with canons from other reforming collections such as the *Decretum* of Burchard and the *Collection in 74 Titles*. Through this combination its currency was maintained in canonistic thought and activity in south and central Italy in its many derivatives. This currency lasted until the middle of the twelfth century, when the *Decretum* of Gratian became the dominant collection of canon law throughout Europe. Nonetheless, there is one derivative collection of the *Collection in Five Books* which was current beyond the *Decretum* of Gratian. The manuscript in which it is found, Montecassino, Archivio dell'Abbazia, 216, has been dated palaeographically to

---

ation allocution,' *Mediaeval Studies* 47 (1985) pp. 438-444; R. Reynolds, 'The South-Italian Canon Law *Collection in Five Books* and its derivatives,' and 'South and Central Italian Canonical Collections of the Tenth and Eleventh Centuries (non-Gregorian).'

8 The critical edition of this collection is by J. T. Gilchrist, *Diversorum patrum sententie sive Collectio in LXXIV titulos digesta.*, Monumenta Iuris Canonici Series B: *Corpus Collectionum* 1 (Vatican City, 1973). For manuscripts of the collection see below, Addendum B, p. 24.

9 The standard editions of parts of the collection are found in Migne, *PL* 149.486-534; and F. Thaner, *Anselmi episcopi Lucensis: Collectio canonum una cum collectione minore iussu Instituti Saviniani* (Innsbruck, 1906-1915; repr. Aalen 1965) [edition, Rec. A, based on Vat. Barb. lat. 535]. And now see K. G. Cushing, *Papacy and Law in the Gregorian Revolution: The Canonistic Work of Anselm of Lucca* (Oxford, 1998). For manuscripts of the collection, see below, Addendum C, p. 25.

10 For manuscripts of the unedited *Tripartita* see below, Addendum D, p. 26.

11 The standard 'edition' of the *Decretum* is found in PL 161. For manuscripts, see below, Addendum E, p. 26.

12 The standard 'edition' of the *Panormia* is found in PL 161. For manuscripts see below, Addendum F, p. 27.

the late twelfth century,[13] and the collection is here entitled the *Collectio canonum Casinensis duodecimi saeculi (codex terscriptus)* because it was likely written at and for Montecassino or one of her dependencies and because the codex itself is a terscriptus one, the canon law collection being written over two earlier erased texts. While the text of the collection itself may have been compiled in the early twelfth century–as its most recent canons might indicate[14]–the facts that the manuscript was copied in the late twelfth century and shows signs of wear indicate the collection's usefulness into a time beyond the compilation of Gratian's *Decretum.*

Whenever the collection was first compiled, the texts within it especially reflect three impulses of ecclesiastical reform in the eleventh-century canon law collections: canons from the south Italian *Collection in Five Books,* Burchard's *Decretum,* some frequently found in the reforming collections of the so-called Gregorian-Reform period, particularly the *Collection in 74 Titles,* and even Ivo's *Decretum.* That the *Collectio canonum Casinensis* should include canons from these three sources is perhaps not surprising inasmuch as there were connections between Montecassino itself and all three of these types of reforming collections.

The *Collection in Five Books* itself was early connected with that great Benedictine monastery. Although the collection may have been compiled elsewhere in southern Italy–perhaps at San Liberatore where the famous reforming abbot of Montecassino, Theobald, had earlier been provost–the earliest and best surviving manuscript of the *Collection in Five Books,* Montecassino Archivio dell'Abbazia 125, was almost certainly copied in Montecassino, probably around the middle of the eleventh century.[15] While there are no canons in the collection that are specifically connected to Montecassino, there are several that may reflect incidents there during the time of the Emperor Henry II.

[13] E. A. Lowe, *The Beneventan Script. A History of the South Italian Minuscule,* 2nd ed. prepared and enlarged by V. Brown, Sussidi Eruditi 33, 34 (Rome, 1980) 2, 76.

[14] On the most recent canon, CCCXXVII of the Lateran Council of 1110, see U.-R. Blumenthal, *The Early Councils of Pope Paschal II 1100-1110,* Studies and Texts 43 (Toronto, 1978) 120; and R. Somerville, *Pope Urban II. The Collectio Britannica and the Council of Melfi (1089)* (Oxford, 1996) 187, n. 3.

[15] See the palaeographical and codicological analysis in Reynolds, 'Southern and Central Italian Collections before the Reform.'

There is first an unusual canon attributed to Henry himself (in our collection attributed to Henry I) in which those who plunder shipwrecks are anathematized.[16] At Montecassino Henry underwent a miraculous cure 'and from that time forward, he studiously served St. Benedict and every practitioner of the monastic life with a special veneration and love, and acted as a benign and devoted father, enriching and protecting the goods of the church.'[17] It was at this time that Henry succeeded in replacing the hellenizing Abbot Atenulf with Theobald, the provost of San Liberatore, which, as Theo Kölzer has suggested, may have had a manuscript of the *Collection in Five Books.*[18] The *Chronicle* of Montecassino reports that Abbot Atenulf fleeing from Henry II to Constantinople perished at sea and that with him went down nine bulls with golden seals, several of which were given by Henry II.[19] For Henry to have anathematized those who would plunder shipwrecks is understandable in such a context. In yet another canon attributed to Henry II there may be reflected another situation at Montecassino. The *Chronicle* of Montecassino notes that on the election of Theobald as abbot, Henry II gave to the monastery many gifts, some of which had been pawned to the Jews and that Henry II and Pope Benedict VIII forbade ecclesiastical goods to be pledged like this.[20] Again, this prohibition may be reflected in a canon attributed to Henry II in the fourth book of *Collection in Five Books,* 'De eo qui pignus vel donum de ornamentis ecclesiae acceperit.'[21]

The *Decretum* of Burchard of Worms is also connected with Montecassino. While that collection was compiled in Germany in the early eleventh century and was especially popular in northern Europe, it quickly was taken into Italy. There are notices as early as the

[16] CCLXXXIII. For another later canon on shipwreck victims, see the canon *Quicumque* of the Lateran Council of 1110, on which see Blumenthal, *The Early Councils of Paschal II,* 120, which appears as canon CCCXXVII of our collection.

[17] H. Hoffmann, *Die Chronik von Montecassino/Chronica monasterii Casinensis,* Monumenta Germaniae Historica, Scriptores 34 (Hannover, 1980) 250.

[18] See Kölzer, *op. cit.* p. 54, n. 128, and Reynolds, 'Southern and Central Italian Collections before the Reform.'

[19] *Die Chronik von Montecassino/Chronica monasterii Casinensis,* 243.

[20] *Die Chronik von Montecassino/Chronica monasterii Casinensis,* 250.

[21] Cf. Montecassino MS 125, p. 247.

1030s that manuscripts of it were at Nonantola;[22] canons from it were early combined with southern Italian canons in such compilations as that in Vatican, Biblioteca Apostolica Vaticana, Vat. lat. 3830;[23] and it provided a major canonistic source in the works of Peter Damian.[24] As for its presence at Montecassino, there are manuscripts of it now there written in both Beneventan and Caroline scripts, Montecassino, Archivio dell'Abbazia, 44 and 45.[25] While it is not beyond all doubt that these manuscripts were copied at Montecassino itself–although both have Beneventan script texts or additions–the existence of many canons from the *Decretum* in our *Collectio canonum Casinensis* and the fact that it specifically cites the *Decretum* and *Corrector* of Burchard indicates that in some form it was known there.

There are connections between Montecassino and such great reforming collections as the *Collection in 74 Titles*. Indeed, it is likely that three of its manuscripts were copied in Montecassino or the near vicinity. The first is Montecassino, Archivio dell'Abbazia, 522.[26] This manuscript of the *Collection in 74 Titles* was written in Beneventan script in the late eleventh or early twelfth century most probably at Montecassino. Its contents have been described by John Gilchrist, who used the text of the *Collection in 74 Titles* therein as one of his primary witnesses.[27] In fact, the codex contains canons from a great variety of sources beyond the *Collection in 74 Titles*. There is a florilegium of texts including the *Collectio Dionysio-Hadriana*, the *Pseudo-Isidorian Decretals*, Burchard, and even Gregory VII, some of which are in the *Collectio canonum Casinensis*. Also there is a florilegium of

[22] See above, n. 4.

[23] See Reynolds, 'Southern and Central Italian Collections before the Reform.'

[24] See above, n. 4.

[25] See Lowe, *The Beneventan Script*, 61. Montecassino, Archivio dell'Abbazia, 45 (saec. XI^2; Montecassino, partially in Beneventan script); and 44 (saec. XI^2; southern Italy; this manuscript is not noted in Lowe as containing Beneventan script, but in fact there is a marginal notation in Beneventan script on p. 265).

[26] On the manuscript see U.-R. Blumenthal, 'A proposito del ms. 522 dell' archivio di Montecassino,' *Benedictina* 22 (1976) 444.

[27] J. T. Gilchrist, *Diversorum patrum sententie sive Collectio in LXXIV titulos digesta.*, Monumenta Iuris Canonici Series B: *Corpus Collectionum* 1 (Vatican City, 1973) lxxxvii.

texts deriving partly from the *Collection in Five Books*.[28] The second of the manuscripts of the *Collection in 74 Titles* is El Escorial, Real Biblioteca de San Lorenzo, L.III.19. Written in Beneventan and Caroline scripts at the end of the eleventh century, possibly at Montecassino, it is unfortunately mutilated and contains the text of the *Collection in 74 Titles* only down to cap. 263. One wonders if the complete text of this manuscript, like Montecassino 522, might not also have had snippets added from the *Collection in Five Books*. Thus, it is significant that in another manuscript now at El Escorial, Z.III.19, there is a further exemplar of the *Collection in 74 Titles* written in Beneventan script of the late eleventh century possibly at Montecassino or the vicinity, and this codex does contain snippets from the *Collection in Five Books* after the *Collection in 74 Titles*. The manuscript itself is a relatively small volume and the texts in Beneventan script have often been written over a palimpsested lower text, whose script has not been determined. The texts from the *Collection in Five Books* are found in a florilegium with synodical, papal, and patristic canons, and are taken from many books of the *Collection in Five Books*. Further, they display monastic features, and Pseudo-Gregorian and Pseudo-Bonifacian texts on monastic privileges, also found in our *Collectio canonum Casinensis*, are included in this miscellany.[29]

Finally, there is a heavy use in our collection of the *Decretum* of Ivo of Chartres or a source like it. While there are no extant manuscripts of this collection at Montecassino, there is evidence that the *Decretum* may have been known in areas where the Beneventan script was written,[30] and it may even have supplied the inscription for the Melfi canon in our collections.[31]

If one compares the *Collectio canonum Casinensis* with other

[28] Pp. 180-196.

[29] J. T. Gilchrist, 'The influence of the monastic forgeries attributed to Pope Gregory I (JE 1951) and Boniface IV (JE 1996),' in *Fälschungen im Mittelalter: Internationaler Kongreß der Monumenta Germaniae Historica, München, 16.-19. September 1986. Teil II: Gefälschte Rechtstexte; Der bestrafte Fälscher*, Monumenta Germaniae Historica: Schriften 33, II (Hannover, 1988) pp. 263-287.

[30] On this see U.-R. Blumenthal, 'An Episcopal Handbook from Twelfth-Century Southern Italy, *Codex Rome, Bibl. Vallicelliana F 54/III*,' in *Studia in honorem Eminentissimi Cardinalis Alphonsi M. Stickler*, ed. R. J. Castillo Lara, Studia et Textus Historiae Iuris Canonici 7 (Rome, 1992) 22.

[31] Somerville, *op. cit.*, 187.

canonical collections, beyond the *Collection in Five Books* itself, still represented in extant manuscripts at Montecassino–for example, the *Collectio Dionysio-Hadriana,*[32] the *Breviatio canonum,*[33] the *Concordia Cresconii,*[34] the *Collectio Vetus Gallica,*[35] the *Dacheriana,*[36] the *Pseudo-Isidorian Decretals,*[37] and Burchard's *Decretum*[38]–the *Collectio canonum Casinensis* is of a special type. The others consist largely of papal and conciliar canons and are directed especially to clerics. The *Collectio canonum Casinensis,* on the other hand, besides containing many of these canons, has canons directed to concerns of the Abbey of Montecassino itself, the papacy, and clerics, religious, and laity. There is a block of canons regarding the abbey, cc. CCCXII through CCCXV. A block of canons with the concerns of the papacy is found grouped together from cc. CCXCI through CCCIV. Then there are at least twenty-four canons directed to monks and nuns, and there is one significant block of canons from cc. CCCV to CCCXV reflecting this concern. But the vast majority of canons deal directly with concerns of clerics and laity–at least 103–with sixty-four regarding women and marriage. In short, despite its lack of system, the *Collectio canonum Casinensis* is a collection specifically for the use of Montecassino or its dependencies in the administration of the abbey and ministration to clerics and lay people, especially in terms of penitential discipline.

The *Collectio canonum Casinensis* is a mixture of what are known as farraginous and Quellenblock collections.[39] Canons have been chosen at random, sometimes as blocks from other collections, sometimes as individual canons. Like many of the collections deriving from the *Collection in Five Books,* the canons from Burchard's *Decretum* represent the heaviest admixture. From Burchard's *Decretum*

[32] MS 522.
[33] MS 541.
[34] MS 541.
[35] MS 372.
[36] MSS 541 and 554.
[37] MS 1.
[38] MSS 44 and 45.
[39] On this see R. Reynolds, 'Law, Canon, before Gratian,' *Dictionary of the Middle Ages*, ed. J. R. Strayer (New York, 1986) 7: 395-413.

(which in its original form contained only nineteen books),[40] canons have been drawn from LL. 1-3, 5-7, and 9-19, LL. 3, 9, and 19 being used especially heavily. Canons from all five books of the *Collection in Five Books* are represented, LL. 4 and 5 being used especially heavily. In the case of both of these early eleventh-century reform collections, the compiler tended to use one source for a block of canons and then skip to the other. The canons from these two sources are found largely in the first part of the collection. With c. CCIV the compiler suddenly turned to canons from the late eleventh century and then returned to Burchard. With cc. CCXXXII and CCXXXIII a source like the florilegium in Montecassino 522 is used, after which come canons largely from Burchard and the *Collection in Five Books*. Canons reflecting high papal prerogatives drawn from the *Proprie auctoritates apostolice sedis* and the *Collection in 74 Titles* form a block beginning in the midst of c. CCXCIX and going through c. CCCXXI. Intruded into this is a block of canons dealing specifically with Montecassino from c. CCCXI through CCCXIV. There are then several papal canons followed by the most recent canons in the collection, those of Urban II and Paschal II in cc. CCCXXVII and CCCXXVIII. The remainder of the collection is drawn largely from Burchard, Ivo's *Decretum*, and the *Collection in Five Books*. It is interesting that most of the canons from c. CCCXXIV to the end of the collection are taken from Burchard, that they are virtually all papal canons, and that the addressees of the pope are specified.

The attributions of the canons (seen in the appendix to the incipit-explicit edition of the collection) are of interest. Often they are incorrect as to the ultimate source, as they are in the *Collection in Five Books* and Burchard. Nontheless, there is a mix of conciliar canons of all types running from the major ecumenical councils to local councils, papal canons from Clement through Paschal II, canons from a variety of non-papal writers, including the emperors Justinian and Henry II (designated as Henry I), penitentials, Burchard's collection specifically so designated, and finally fifty canons without attributions.

[40] See H. Hoffmann and R. Pokorny, *Das Dekret des Bischofs Burchard von Worms: Textstufen, frühe Verbreitung, Vorlagen*, Monumenta Germaniae Historica: Hilfsmittel, 12 (Munich, 1991).

As to the compiler of the collection, like many early medieval collections there is no indication of authorship in the text itself, although a modern hand has noted that it may have been a certain Arialdus Presbyter, mentioned by Peter the Deacon in the *De viris illustribus*, c. 22.[41] But this reference does not mean he was the author of our collection. In a necrology of Montecassino, MS 47, fol. 185v, one does find a certain Arialdus mentioned as dying on II Kal. Apr. before the middle of the twelfth century, but he is cited as a deacon.[42]

Codicological and Palaeographical Description

The *Collectio canonum Casinensis* is a collection of canon law material, the most recent canon dating to the twelfth century. The text itself was written in the late twelfth century, according to E. A. Lowe and Virginia Brown, thus making it the youngest canon law collection written in Beneventan script, together with the late twelfth-century fragment of Gratian's *Decretum* in the Biblioteca dell'Abbazia of Montevergine, Perg. 6518.[43]

The current shelfmark of the *Collectio canonum Casinensis* is 216, but there are older marks: Lit^{a} N:6 (in pen), O (in pen), and 150/100 (in pencil) on the front flyleaf; S20 (in pen on the spine); at the base of p. 1 is the familiar sixteenth-century ex libris: 'Iste liber est sacri monasterii Casinen. N° 660'; on p. 3 (fol. 2r) at the bottom a modern cursive hand reads: 'Institucione sanctorum patrum et qualitate colparum (*sic*).' The manuscript appears to be complete and homogen-

[41] PL 173.1033: 'Arialdus Casinensis presbyter scripsit eleganti sermone quosdam tractatus; fuit autem eo tempore quo et Albericus.'

[42] I am grateful to Professor Charles Hilken for information on Arialdus. The necrology of Montecassino, MS 47 has the name Arialdus once on 31 March. This same notice appears in two other necrologies related to the community at Montecassino, the liturgical calendar/necrology of Cardinal Leo of Ostia (Vatican, BAV Borg. 211) and the necrology of San Nicola della Cicogna (Montecassino MS 179). In all three Arialdus is called a *diaconus* or *levita*. There do not seem to be necrological notices for an Arialdus *sacerdos*.

[43] See R. Reynolds, 'Gratian's *Decretum* and the *Code* of Justianian in Beneventan Script' (Miscellanea beneventana 9, Juridica), *Mediaeval Studies* 58 (1996) 285-288.

eous. The incipit and explicit of fol. 2 read: '... grinos inter virgines ... dei non alii ut.'

The manuscript has a post-medieval binding of undetermined age. The rectangular boards, measuring 164 x 107 mm, are of wood and are squared; there is a crack on the front cover along the spine. The boards are fully covered with a white to light-brown parchment that is partially worn. The spine is flat and divided by three single thick bands. In the upper sector is written 'O' and '216'; in the second and third sectors in light brown ink: 'Incertus de disciplina sacerdotum et qualitate culparum M.S.;' and in the lowest sector 'S20.'

The quires of the codex are sewn with brown thread. There are two sets of binding holes, the current ones and four older ones. From the top of the codex the current holes measure 42, 80, 120, and 145 mm and the four original holes 20, 61, 105, and 138 mm.

There is a paper front pastedown measuring 155 x 107 mm, on which is written in a modern cursive hand under the current ex libris label 'Recensetur inter codices exscriptas tempore abbatis ... suspicarisis ... Leo ... 63.' This suggests perhaps that the manuscript was one of those reported by Leo in his *Chronicle* to have been copied in the abbacy of Desiderius. Obviously the date of the script is against this. The paper rear pastedown measures 155 x 102 mm. Partially attached to the front pastedown is an unpaginated paper flyleaf measuring 153 x 102 mm. After the older shelfmarks on the flyleaf is a description of the contents of the collection: 'Codex Seculi XI continet Institutionem Sanctorum Patrum de qualitate culparum, et de disciplina, atque doctrina Sacerdotum, quae Institutio authorem habuisse videtur Monachum quemdam Casinensem, qui floruerit post annum 1080. ex Bullis Pontificum Romanorum ab eo relatis pag. 91 et 92 Ioannis IX Ragemprando Abbati Casinensis, Sergii III Leoni similiter Abb. Casin. Leonis IX Richerio Abb. Casin. et ex decreto Gregorii VII contra Normannos. Anne ejus auctor, vel compilator dici, MS picarique poterit Arialdus Casinensis Presbyter, de quo Petrus Diaconus de Viri Illustr. Casinensis p. 22.' Attached to the back pastedown is a blank, unpaginated paper flyleaf measuring 157 x 101 mm.

Together with the modern pagination numbers in the outer lower corners of the pages, which will be used in the current description of the codex, there are at least two or three other types of foliation/pagination: (1) one type of foliation is in ink at the upper outer folios from 1-63; (2) another foliation in ink in the upper right corner on 71, 76, 89, 90, 91; (3) what is fol. 89 has a '90' in dark black ink and '179' in pencil in the upper right hand corner; (4) on page 180 in the upper left corner in pencil is '180'; (5) on page 183 there is written 'p. 181' in the upper right corner next to '91'; (6) on page 199 in the upper right in black ink is '100'; (7) on page 223 in the upper right corner in black ink, but of a different hand than the others in black ink pagination is '112'; (8) on page 224 in the upper left corner is 'p. 224.' All of the numerals, which are in the upper or lower outside corners of the folios, are arabic and are modern.

There are fourteen quires, each consisting of four bifolia, and each with normal hair-flesh organization (i.e., hffhhffhhffhhffh). The folios of good quality and medium thickness and measuring 153 x 110 mm have been trimmed, thereby destroying what may have been signatures and catchwords. Some folios still bear traces of the rubrical instructions now included in the text itself.

Most pages are very heavily scraped, and on some there are clearly older texts erased. The pages where older texts are still visible are: 13-14, 17-18, 22 (clearly the text lines running opposite the upper-most text), 23-24, 26, 27 (text with some larger letters running opposite the upper-most text), 30 (text running opposite the upper-most text), 31 (text running opposite the upper-most text), 40, 42, 46 (text running opposite the upper-most text) 48, 49, 50, 53 (text in Beneventan script running opposite the upper-most text), 55 (double set of line prickmarks), 72 (double set of line prickmarks), 126 (text running opposite the upper-most text), 129, 162 (conjoint with 175, which certainly has an older text), 166 (conjoint with 171, which has an older text), 175 in the margin, where someone has added a reagent to bring up the text, which is certainly in Beneventan script), 181 (clearly has erased text running in the same direction on extra lines: conjoint with 187/188 that clearly have older text in the same direction as the upper-most text), 190 (with text in the opposite direction to the upper-most text), 193 (with text in the same direction as the upper-most text), 194 (with musical notation), 195, 196 (very clear lower text with script running opposite to the upper-most text), 198 (conjoint with 203, which has text running in the same direction as upper-most text), 199 (which still has a set of line prickmarks across the bottom of the folio and double prickmarks in the margin, suggesting a codex terscriptus), 200, 201 (like 199), 202 (almost certainly a codex terscriptus; there are the double marginal prickmarks and the bottom prickmarks, and visible are erased letters running both opposite to and in the same direction as the upper-most text; also on the opposite p. 201, with the same prickmark system there appears to be a rubric running in the opposite direction), 203, 205, 213 (conjoint with 219 with double set of line prickmarks and line prickmarks on the bottom of the folio), 215 (conjoint with 218; 215 has drypoint text lines running opposite the upper-most script), 216, 217, 218, 219. The following pages have double line prickmarks (and others have almost certainly disappeared in trimming): 17-18, 23, 27, 39, 41, 45, 51, 55, 65, 71, 73, 79, 81, 85, 91, 95, 143, 183, 189, 191, 199, 201, 211, 213, 219. The following pages have more lines or prickmarks drawn than are used in the upper-most text: 9, 11, 15, 17, 19, 21, 23, 25, 27, 29, 31, 115, 119, 121, 125, 129, 133, 139, 143, 145, 147, 149, 151, 153, 155, 157, 159, 161, 163, 167, 169, 171, 173, 175, 177, 179, 181, 183, 185, 187, 189, 191, 193, 199, 201, 211, 213, 219. On page 23, the letters 'l' and 'm' of the lower script are very thin, unusual even for early Beneventan script, reminding one of Visigothic letters. The codex was a practical one, not deluxe, and it bears evidence of use. Some folios are worn, but they do not show the heavy use evident in the Montecassino codex of the *Collection in Five Books,* MS 125. It is noteworthy that unlike many other collections deriving from the *Collection in Five Books,* this one has no glossed words, although at times the gloss in the *Collection in Five Books* has been used rather than the original word itself.

In the layout of the codex prickmarks from both fleshside to hairside and hairside to fleshside were made using both holes and slits. In the outer and inner margins there are one or two marginal prickmarks; when there are two they are ca. 8 mm apart. Those in the outer margin are 18 and 23 mm from the side of the folio, 5 mm from the top of the folio, and 2 mm from the bottom. The ruling for the 18 or 19 lines on each folio of this single-column manuscript has been made in drypoint. The written space of the folios is ca. 120 mm from the bottom rule to the headline of the minims. The horizontal measurement between marginal rules is ca. 80 mm, and the measurement between rules is ca. 6 to 7 mm.

The text is written in brown/black ink by a single hand. Minims are 2.5 mm, and ascenders and descenders 4.5 mm. Rubrics in red measure ca. 21 to 22 mm and are placed over the text. Intials from ca. 6 to 10 mm are written in the outer left-hand margin in a red majuscule with green and/or yellow infill. Capital letters written within the text are in a brown/black ink and measure from ca. 4 to 6 mm.

The script is very angular, suggesting a later date. Characteristic letters are a double-diamond 'd'; 'o' often looks like an 'a'; and the upper stroke of 't' goes up and that of 'a' goes down. Ligatures and joined letters are normal for Beneventan script of Montecassino of the late twelfth century, and noticeable are the double 'd's,' and the 'o' and 'a' in words like 'Romana' and 'Magotiensis,' which must be read as 'Romano' and Mogatiensis.' There are some ticks over words, especially monosyllabic words and over 'i's,' a late sign probably reflecting an earlier source with a circumflex. Abbreviations using contractions, suspensions, superscript, and special signs are frequent, and nomina sacra are also used. Numerals in the text are Roman. Medial stops may be a point or a point with a tick over it. A final stop may be a point or a tilda with a stroke under it. Corrections, consisting of letters above the word corrected, are rare. On the blank space at the conclusion of the manuscript, a Beneventan hand of the late twelfth century has added an *Oratio sancti Augustini episcopi,* which has been made virtually illegible through the use of a reagent to bring up the text.

There have been two support fragments written in a stately eleventh-century Beneventan hand bound into the manuscript, one between pp. 16 and 17, and the other between pp. 208 and 209. The one between pp. 16 and 17 could be seen in a microfilm of the manuscript used in 1985, but as of June, 1995, it had gone missing, although a tiny portion is still attached to the binding threads. The measurements of the fragment between pp. 208 and 209 are 152 x 17 mm. The ink is brown/black. Lines are 10 mm apart. Minims are 3.5 mm and ascenders and descenders are 8 mm. The following words or sets of letters can be seen on the two fragments:

PP. 16-17 RECTO	PP. 16-17 VERSO	PP. 208-209 RECTO	PP. 208-209 VERSO
ad	To	eam	usa
ivi r	ino	gite	nos e
quos	g	nec su	eius et
vulg	a uns	te ur	gus
runt qu	ione	occis	asi
d th	temp	eorum	esau
ccit	fugi	Vox	as
cresce	a bo	deter	ent
ea inp	hii	in sy	orten
c ho	oli eius	temp	cbi
tui	pluri	lone	sfica
ruti	con	cum	ones
uet	lus	et vul	que in
uea	uum	opus si	ur

These words are from Jeremiah 50. 26-29 and 35-39, and the strips appear to be cut from the outside corners of a large two-column Bible, such as one currently found in the *Compactio I* at Montecassino. According to Virginia Brown, who will do a study of the remains of this Bible, there is a fragment of a Missal from Galatina in Puglia by the same scribe or made in the same center.

Comments on Editorial Principles

Capitulatio numbers in ⟨ ⟩ have been added to facilitate consultation. They correspond to the rubrics given in the manuscript. In some places there are 'sub-capitulationes' within a capitulatio. In such cases the sub-capitulatio is not assigned a number. Rubrics and attributions in capital letters reflect the rubrication in the manuscript. Parentheses ( ) around a letter signify a correction of that letter by the scribe.

Spelling in Beneventan-script codices is notoriously inconsistent and faulty.[44] In this incipit-explicit edition spelling in the manuscript has been maintained[45] since spellings here may suggest relationships with other derivative collections based on the *Collection in Five Books* or other canonical collections used by the compilers of the Cassino collection. In almost all cases throughout the manuscript 'e' is used for 'ae,' so here also this practice has been followed.

Following the lead of the CD Rom program by Linda Fowler-Magerl, *Kanones. A Selection of Canon Law Collections Compiled Outside Italy Between 1000 and 1140,*[46] the incipits/explicits reported here consist of a minimum of six words. There has usually been an attempt to maintain integral syntactical units. Occasionally more than six words must be used to distinguish canons with the same or similar first six words or canons that begin by stating their source, such as a council. Roman numerals have been maintained unless a suprascript letter has been added, in which case they have been expanded (e.g., i^{m} > unum; iii^{s} > tres, etc.)

Sources for the canons are assigned as follows. Canons taken from Burchard's *Decretum* are cited not from the superior edition of M. de Neuss [Novesianus] (Cologne, 1548; reprinted with introductory essays by T. Kölzer and G. Fransen [Aalen, 1992]), but according to the Migne 'edition,' (PL 140), because of ease of consultation. Canons from Ivo's *Decretum* (= Dec.) and *Panormia* (= Pan.) are cited from the 'editions' in PL 161. Canons from the *Collection in Five Books,* LL 1-3, are cited from Mario Fornasari's edition, *Collectio canonum in v libris (Lib. i-iii), (Corpus christianorum, Continuatio Mediaevalis* 6; Turnhout, 1970) (= Forn.), with the pagination also from the Montecassino manuscript of that collection (C = Montcassino MS 125) inasmuch as Fornasari's text varies at times from that manuscript; even though in some cases (e.g., CXIV) the Vatican manuscript, Vatican, Biblioteca Apostolica Vaticana, Vat. lat 1339, used by

[44] On this see R. Jacobsson, 'Short Reflexions on Beneventan Easter Sequence Texts,' *La Sequenza Medievale, Atti del Convegno Internazionale Milano 7-8 aprile 1984,* ed. A. Ziino (Lucca, 1992) 129 f.

[45] On the importance of maintaining the original spelling of manuscripts in editions of medieval texts, see the comments of Paul Meyvaert in a review appearing in *Speculum* 72 (1997) 527 f.

[46] (Kanones WIP Verlag: Piesenkofen in the Oberpfalz, 1998).

Fornasari has canons that are not in the Montecassino manuscript.[47] Canons from the *Collection in Five Books,* LL 4-5 are cited from the Montecassino manuscript of the collection inasmuch as the Vatican and Vallicelliana manuscripts of the collection (Vatican, Biblioteca Apostolica Vaticana, Vat. lat 1339; and Rome, Biblioteca Vallicelliana, B 11) are defective. Canons from the *Collection in 74 Titles* are cited from the critical edition of J. T. Gilchrist, *Diuersorum patrum sententie siue Collectio in LXXIV titulos digesta,* Monumenta iuris canonici, Ser. B: Corpus collectionum 1 (Vatican City, 1973). Canons found in *Italia pontificia* are cited from *Italia pontificia; sive, Repertorium privilegiorum et litterarum a romanis pontificibus ante annum 1598 Italiae ecclesiis, monasteriis, civitatibus singulisque personis concessorum*, ed. P. F. Kehr (Berlin, 1906-1935). Canons from the *Paenitentiale Vallicellianum I* (found in Rome, Biblioteca Vallicelliana E 15, [saec. XI/XII in part in Beneventan script]) are cited from H. J. Schmitz, *Die Bussbücher und die Bussdisciplin der Kirche,* 1 (Mainz, 1883). Sources of other canons, when known, and parallels to other manuscripts at Montecassino (e.g., MSS 1, 44, 45, 215 Z, 439, 522, 541, 554) are cited from appropriate documents. It would be possible for many canons to cite parallels given in Fowler-Magerl's *Kanones*, but in light of the almost consistent use of canons found in the *Collection in Five Books*, Burchard, and Ivo's *Decretum*, such citations would clutter the apparatus fontium unnecessarily and can easily be found by using *Kanones.* Other abbreviations for citations are:

Blumenthal = U.-R. Blumenthal, *The Early Councils of Pope Paschal II 1100-1110*, Studies and Texts 43 (Toronto, 1978)
Bonizo = *Liber de vita christiana* ed E. Perels (Berlin, 1930)
Caspar = E. Caspar, *Das Register Gregors VII,* Monumenta Germaniae historia. Epistolae selectae 2 (Berlin, 1920)
Deusdedit = *Die Kanonessammlung des Kardinals Deusdedit*, ed. W. von Glanvell (Paderborn 1905; repr. Aalen, 1967).
Gratian = *Corpus iuris canonici*, ed. E. Friedberg (Leipzig, 1879)

[47] That there were manuscripts with the *Collection in Five Books* in forms like that in Vat. lat. 1339 written in Beneventan script is probable since Vat. lat. 1339 has signs that point to an exemplar in Beneventan script.

Hinschius = *Decretales pseudo-Isidorianae et capitula Angilramni*, ed. P. Hinschius (Leipzig, 1863)

Somerville = R. Somerville, *Pope Urban II. The Collectio Britannica and the Council of Melfi (1089)* (Oxford, 1996)

Weiland = *Constitutiones et acta publica imperatorum et regum,* Monumenta Germaniae historica. Legum sectio 4 (Hannover, 1893)

ADDENDA

A. Manuscripts of the *Decretum* of Burchard (see above, n. 4)

Angers, St-Aubin, shelfmark unknown (saec. XII) [missing]; Arras, St-Vaast, shelfmark unknown (saec. XII) [missing]; Assisi, Biblioteca Comunale, 227 (saec. XII) [Bks. XVII-XIX]; Bamberg, Staatsbibliothek, Can. 6 (P.I.5) (saec. XI; Worms); Bamberg, Michelsberg (cf. P. Ruf. *Mittelalterliche Bibliothekskataloge Deutschlands und der Schweiz: Bistümer Augsburg, Bamberg und Eichstätt* [Munich, 1939] 3.3, p. 378; perhaps part now in the Würzburg fragment); Bayeux, Cap. Bibl., shelfmark unknown (1436: *Catalogue général des manuscrits des Bibliothèques Publiques de France, Départements* [Paris, 1889] 10, p. 282 nrs. 130, 132) [missing]; Bec, shelfmark unknown (2 mss., both saec. XII; one used by Philippe of Bayeux before 1142; one listed in the saec. XII catalogue as 128, the other in the Philippe Harcourt register as 49; cf. G. Becker, *Catalogi bibliothecarum antiqui* [Bonn, 1885-1887, repr. Hildesheim, 1973], pp. 200, nr. 47; and 265, nr. 125) [missing]; Berlin, Staatsbibliothek zu Berlin, Phill. 92 (olim 1778) (saec. XII; Poitiers) [excerpts]; Besançon, Bibliothèque Diocésaine, shelfmark unknown (cf. J. Boehmer, *Corpus iuris canonici* 1 [Halle, 1747] p. 1239) [missing]; Bologna, Biblioteca Universitaria, 2239 (Cat. 1107) (saec. XI; Italy); and 2599 (Cat. 1358) (saec. XII) [excerpts, Bks. I-XV]; Bologna, Collegio di Spagna, 37 (saec. XII½; Italy); Bordeaux, Bibliothèque Municipale, 11 (saec. XI-XII); Bordeaux, Cathedral (cf. J. Boehmer, *Corpus iuris canonici* [Halle, 1747] 1, p. 1239); Bruxelles, Bibliothèque Royale Albert Ier, 3819-20 (Cat. 2499) (saec. XII; St. Matthias, Trier); Burgo de Osma, Biblioteca del Cabildo, 157 (246) (saec. XI-XII); Chartres, Bibliothèque Municipale, 161 (154) [partially destroyed]; and 234 [Bk. XIX]; Cheltenham, Phillipps Collection (saec. XIex; mentioned by H. Schenkl, *Bibliotheca Patrum latinorum Britannica* [Vienna, 1892] I.2, p. 153); Cluny, shelfmark unknown (saec. XII) (cf. L. Delisle, *Inventaire des manuscrits de la Bibliothèque Nationale, Fonds de Cluni* [Paris, 1884] p. 365, nr. 434) [missing]; Cortona, Biblioteca Comunale e dell'Accademia Etrusca, 75 (XII1/2; central Italy); Cremona, Biblioteca della Cattedrale, shelfmark unknown (catalogue of 1201, mentioned by O. Meyer, 'Überlieferung und Verbreitung des Dekrets des Bischofs Burchard von Worms,' *Zeitschrift der Savigny-Stiftung für Rechtsgeschichte, Kanonistische Abteilung* 24 [1935] p. 149.) [missing]; Dresden, Sächsische Landesbibliothek, A.118 (saec. XII; Herzogenburg) [excerpts]; Durham, Cathedral Library, shelfmark unknown (saec. XI) (cf. Becker, *Catalogi bibliothecarum antiqui*, p. 240, nrs. 80+81] [missing]; Durham, Cathedral Library, B.IV.17 (saec. XII; Durham); Eichstätt, Universitätsbibliothek, st. 772 (olim Bibliothek des Domkapitels,

48, olim 6) (a. 1040 x 1050; Bavaria/Franken); El Escorial, Real Biblioteca de San Lorenzo, d.I.1 (later addition to saec. X ms.) [fragment]; d.III.7 (saec. XVI) [fragment]; and T.I.14 (saec. XI); Fécamp, shelfmark unknown (114 in saec. XII catalogue.); Firenze, Biblioteca Medicea Laurenziana, 16.21 (saec. XI-XII; central Italy, Fontibene); 7.1 (saec. XI; Santa Croce) [abridgement]; and Calci 9 (olim 60) (saec. XI$^{1/4}$; Tuscany, provenance Pisa); Firenze, Biblioteca Nazionale Centrale, Conv. soppr. C.I.2777 (Badia Fior.) (saec. XI-XII; Italian: provenance S. Giustina Padua) [excerpt]; and Conv. soppr. F.IV.255 (Vallombrosa); Firenze, Biblioteca Riccardiana, 240 (saec. XI-XII); Fleury (cf. *Notices et extraits des manuscrits de la Bibliothèque Nationale et autres bibliothèques* [Paris, 1884] 31.1, p. 432, nr. 129); Frankfurt am Main, Stadt- und Universitätsbibliothek, Barth. 50 (saec. XI$^{1/4}$; Worms); and fragment lat. I.34 (saec. XII); Freiburg i. Breisgau, Universitätsbibliothek, 7 (saec. XI: 1034x1046; Constance); Fulda, cod. fragment 4 (nr. 73) (saec. XII$^{4/4}$; provenance Fulda); Fulda (saec. XV-XVI), shelfmark unknown (cf. K. Christ, *Die Bibliothek des Klosters Fulda* [Leipzig, 1933] pp. 109, 256, 299); Genève, Bibliothèque et Universitaire, shelfmark unknown (1035-1070: J. Senebier, *Catalogue raisonné des manuscrits conservés dans la bibliothèque de la ville et république de Genève* [Geneva, 1779] p. 57) [missing]; 's-Gravenhage, Rijksmuseum Meermanno-Westreenianum, 10.D.21 (saec. XI/XII; northern France) [fragment]; Hannover, Hauptstaatsarchiv Dep. 76, Heine-Halberstadt MS 44, Mappe 2, Nr. 14 (saec. XI^{2}; provenance Halberstadt); Ivrea, Biblioteca Capitolare, LXXII [the manuscript may contain Burchard or may be a manuscript of Gratian]; and XCIV (saec. XI$^{4/4}$; provenance Ivrea); København, Kongelike Bibliothek, Gl. kgl. S. 1617 4° (saec. XII^{in}; provenance Minden, St. Martin) [excerpts]; Köln, Erzbischöfliche Diözesan- und Dombibliothek, 119 (saec. XI$^{1/4}$; Worms); Konstanz, Dom (cf. P. Lehmann, *Mittelalterliche Bibliothekskataloge Deutschlands und der Schweiz* [Munich, 1918] 1, p. 196); Lambach, Bibliothek des Benediktinerstifts, Cml. XVI (saec. XI^{ex}); Leiden, Bibliotheek van de Rijksuniversiteit, uncataloged fragment; Leipzig, Universitätsbibliothek, Cod. 60, fols. 81-94 (Bk. XIX); Liège (St-Laurent, catalogue of saec. XII/XIII; cf. R. van Caeneghem, 'Notes on canon law books in medieval Belgian booklists,' *Studia Gratiana* 12 [1967] p. 270, n. 10); Limoges, St-Martial, shelfmark unknown (saec. XII-XIII) (cf. L. Delisle, *Le Cabinet des manuscrits de la Bibliothèque (impériale) nationale: Etude sur la formation de ce dépôt comprenant les éléments d'une histoire de la calligraphie, de la miniature, de la reliure, et du commerce des livres à Paris avant l'invention de l'imprimerie* [Paris 1868-81, repr. 1969], 2, p. 494, nr. 80) [missing]; Lisboa, Biblioteca Nacional, Alcobaça 365 (saec. XII$^{4/4}$; Alcobaça); London, British Library, Cotton Claudius C.VI (1070-1089; soon after death of Lanfranc of Canterbury; Canterbury?); and Add. 18371 (saec. XII/XIII, provenance St.

Georgenberg, Fiecht) (Bks. XIX-XX); Los Angeles, University of California Research Library, Department of Special Collections, Collection of Loose Leaves 1/XI/ITA/15 (saec. XI; northern Italy); Lucca, Biblioteca Capitolare Feliniana, 124 (saec. XI^2; central Italy); and 597 (saec. $XI^{4/4}$; central Italy); Lyon, Bibliothèque de la Cathédrale, shelfmark unknown (catalogue of 1085-1106; cf. L. Niepce, *Les bibliothèques anciennes et modernes de Lyon* [Lyons, 1876] p. 585) [missing]; Madrid, Biblioteca Nacional, 386 (olim Biblioteca del Palacio, C.6) (saec. XI-XII); 391 (olim Biblioteca del Palacio, C.7) (saec. XII); and 6367 (a. 1105) (Bk. XX); Maillezais, shelfmark unknown (saec. XII^{ex}) (cf. Delisle, *Le Cabinet des manuscrits de la Bibliothèque (impériale) nationale*, 2, p. 507, nr. 69) [missing]; Mainz, Dom (catalogue of saec. XVIII; cf. H. Hoffmann and R. Pokorny, *Das Dekret des Bischofs Burchard von Worms: Textstufen, frühe Verbreitung, Vorlagen* [*Monumenta Germaniae Historica: Hilfsmittel*, 12; Munich, 1991] p. 160, n. 131); Manchester, John Rylands Library of the University of Manchester, 42 (saec. XI; Germany?) [excerpts]; and 96 (saec. $XII^{1/4}$; middle Italy, Tuscany?); Mantova, Biblioteca Comunale, D.IV.15 (461) (saec. XI^{in}; San Benedetto Polirone); Marburg, Hessisches Staatsarchiv, Hr. 8 fasc. 14 (saec. XII^2; fragment, saec. XI); Milano, Biblioteca Ambrosiana, E.144.sup. (saec. XI; provenance Milan); Milano, Archivio Storico Civico e Biblioteca Trivulziana, 601 (saec. XI; Santa Croce Novara); Modena, Biblioteca Capitolare, O.II.15 (post a. 1052); Montecassino, Archivio dell'Abbazia, 44 (saec. XI^2; Montecassino); and 45 (saec. XI^2; southern Italy); Montpellier, Bibliothèque de la ville, 7 (saec. XI-XII; St-Bernard de Romans); Monza, Biblioteca Capitolare, C-1/61; D-10/152 (olim T.II.212) (saec. XI^2; Italy); and H-5/154 (olim T.IV.214) (saec. XI; northern Italy); München, Bayerische Staatsbibliothek, Clm. 2593 (saec. XIII) [excerpts]; Clm. 3909 (a. 1138x1143; Augsburg or vicinity) [*Statuta canonum de officio sacerdotum*]; Clm. 4570 (20 March 1108; Chur, Benediktbeuren); Clm. 5801c (saec. XII; Ebersberg); Clm. 18094 (saec. XII; provenance Tegernsee); and Clm. 28911 (saec. XII); München, Universitätsbibliothek, 2° 292 (saec. XI^2; middle Italy: Porto, Rome); Napoli, Biblioteca Nazionale Vittorio Emanuele II, Vind. lat. 23 (olim Wien 2044) (saec. $XII^{1/4}$; central Italy, provenance S. Giustina, Padua) [fragment]; Napoli, San Severino (catalogue of saec. XVIII; cf. B. de Montfaucon, *Bibliotheca bibliothecarum manuscriptorum nova* [Paris, 1739; repr. Hildesheim, 1981] 1, p. 233); Nijmegen, Bibliotheek van de Katholieke Universiteit, 185 (saec. XI/XIII; Germany); Nonantola, San Silvestro, (three manuscripts numbered 11, 142, 151; cf. inventory anno post 1035; invent. anno 1331: no. 40; cf. J. Ruysschaert, *Les manuscrits de l'Abbaye de Nonantola*, p. 38) [missing]; Novara, Biblioteca Capitolare, XV [30] (saec. $XII^{1/2}$; Novara) [excerpts Bks. I-III]; and XXVIII [Cat. 17] (alternatively cited as XXVII) (saec. XI; Italy); Orléans, Bibliothèque Municipale, 229

(200) (Fleury); Oxford, St. John's College, 125 (saec. XII) [this ms. is catalogued as Ivo of Chartres, and may contain Ivo rather than Burchard, or, as stated by Z. Brooke, *The English church and the papacy from the conquest to the reign of John* (Cambridge 1931), pp. 237-239, it may be an Ivo ms. containing a Burchard fragment or excerpt]; Paderborn, perhaps Dombibliothek, shelfmark unknown (saec. XII^{med}; cf. Meyer, *art. cit.* p. 149) [missing]; Padova, Biblioteca del Seminario Vescovile, 529 (saec. XI; Italy, San Benedetto Polirone; S. Giustina Padua); Padova, S. Guistina (cf. Migne, *PL* 56.321 or *PL* 140.498) [missing]; Paris, Bibliothèque Nationale, lat. 3861 (saec. XII; provenance Le Puy); lat. 3862 (Colbert 898) (saec. XII$^{2/4}$; central Italy); lat. 3863 (Colbert 415) (saec. XII); lat. 4283 (saec. XII; a Pithou ms.) [excerpts]; lat. 8922 (saec. XI; provenance Echternach) [abridgement]; lat. 9630 (saec. XII$^{1/4}$; Tuscany, provenance Fréjus); lat. 11578 (saec. XII; St-Germain-des-Prés; St-Maur-des-Fossés) [fragment]; lat. 12449 (saec. XII^{1}; Séguier, Coislin, St-Germain-des-Prés); lat. 13659 (saec. XI) [excerpts]; and lat. 14869; Parma, Biblioteca Nazionale Palatina, Parm. 3777 (saec. XI; Italy); Parma, Biblioteca Nazionale Palatina, shelfmark unknown, may be Parm. 3777 supra (post 1077); Pistoia, Archivio Capitolare del Duomo, C.125 (olim C.XII) (saec. XII$^{1/4}$; Pistoia); and C.140 (olim C.XIII) (saec. XII$^{1/4}$; Pistoia); Polirone, San Benedetto Po (cf. Migne, *PL* 56.321 and *PL* 140.498); Pommersfelden, Gräflich Schönborn'sche Bibliothek, 198 (2816) 4° [fragment]; Porto, Cat. Bibl., shelfmark unknown (saec. XI; cf. H. Mordek, 'Bemerkungen zum mittelalterlichen Schatzverzeichnis von Porto/Rom.' *Studia Gratiana* 20 [1976] pp. 233-40) [missing]; Prato, Biblioteca Roncioniana, Q.VIII.4 (3) (saec. XII$^{1/4}$; Pistoia); Ravenna, Archivio vescovado (see Bethmann, *Archiv* 12 [1872-74] 583; perhaps the manuscript at Padova); Reims, Bibliothèque Municipale, 673 (G 522) (provenance St-Remi); 674 (G 523) (1069x1080; or 1096x1106; St-Remi); and 678; Roma, Biblioteca Vallicelliana, A 20 (saec. XII$^{1/4}$; Umbrian/Roman); Roma, Biblioteca Vittorio Emmanuele, Sessor. CXLVII (2034) (saec. XII) [excerpts]; and Varia 398 (3949) (saec. XI) [excerpt]; Rouen, Bibliothèque Municipale, 704, fols. 94-150 (saec. XII, Abbaye de Jumièges) [excerpts]; St-André de Villeneuve près d'Avignon, shelfmark unknown (catalogue of 1307; cf. Delisle, *Le Cabinet des manuscrits de la Bibliothèque (impériale) nationale,* 3, p. 7, nr.7) [missing]; St-Omer, Bibliothèque Municipale, 194 (saec. XII^{2}; provenance St-Omer); St-Pons de Thomières, shelfmark unknown (catalogue of 1276; Delisle, *Le Cabinet des manuscrits de la Bibliothèque (impèriale) nationale,* 2, p. 541, nr. 55) [missing]; Sankt Gallen, Stiftsbibliothek, 674 (saec. XI^{2}); 676 (saec. XI) [*Statuta canonum de officio sacerdotum*]; and 1398a (saec. XII^{1}); Schwabach, Kirchenbibliothek, 7/14 (Cl. 42) fols. 178v-185r (a. 1429) [Bk. XIX]; Siena, Archivio di Stato, A-191 (82) fols. 1-16 (saec. XI) [fragment]; Speyer, Dombibliothek, shelfmark un-

known (cf. P. Lehmann, *Erforschung des Mittelalters,* 2 [Munich, 1959] p. 221) [missing]; Stuttgart, Württembergische Landesbibliothek, HB.VI.107 (saec. XI^{ex}; Constance, St. Blasien, or Schaffhausen) [*Statuta canonum de officio sacerdotum*]; Tarragona, Biblioteca Provincial, 35 (18) (saec. $XII^{1/4}$; ca. a. 1125; Santa Creus) [excerpts]; Torino, Biblioteca Nazionale Universitaria, K.V.9 [fragment, burned 1904]; Troyes, Bibliothèque Municipale, 1386 (saec. XII; Oratoire de Troyes, fonds Pithou): Vaticano, Città del, Biblioteca Apostolica Vaticana, Vat. lat. 1355 (saec. XI; central Italy); Vat. lat. 1356 (saec. XI-XII; central Italy) [fragment]; Vat. lat. 3809 (saec. XI^{2}; central Italy); Vat. lat. 4227 (saec. XI) [Bk. XIX]; Vat. lat. 4880 (saec. XI-XII; central Italy); Vat. lat. 4980, fols. 1-75 (saec. XII^{in}; Italy) [fragment]; Vat. lat. 4980, fol. 76 (ca. 1100) [fragment]; Vat. lat. 4981 (saec. XIII; south Italy) [fragment]; Vat. lat. 7790 (saec. XII^{in}; central Italy); Vat. lat. 14731 (olim Caiazzo) (saec. XI^{ex}; Caiazzo); Arch. San Pietro B. 41 ($XII^{1/2}$; Italy) [fragment]; Barb. lat. 1450 (saec. XI; central Italy, provenance San Salvatore di Montamiata); Pal. lat. 585 and 586 (before a. 1023; Worms, provenance Heidelberg); Reg. lat. 979 (saec. XI^{ex}; Flanders, provenance Brugge); and Urb. lat. 180 (saec. XI; northern Italy); Vercelli, Biblioteca Capitolare Eusebiana, XLI (11) (saec. XI-XII; Italy) [fragment]; XCIV (59) (saec. X-XI; Burchard saec. XI); Vic, Archivo Capitular, fragmenta XV (saec. XII) [fragment]; and fragmenta sin. num. (saec. XII); Wolfenbüttel, Herzog-August-Bibliothek, 32 (35) Helmst. (saec. XI; Hildesheim) [excerpts]; 404.5 (8) Novi (saec. $XI^{1/2}$; Wissembourg) [excerpts]; Wolfenbüttel, Niedersächsisches Staatsarchiv, Mappe 12, Sig. 5 (saec. $XI^{3/4}$; Hildesheim?) [excerpts]; Würzburg, Universitätsbibliothek, Mp.j.f.15 (saec. $XI^{2/4}$; Bamberg) [fragment]; Mp.j.q.2 [excerpts]; Mp.th.f.86 (St. Stefan Würzburg); and Mp.th.f.167 (saec. $XI^{3/4}$; German, provenance Amorbach).

Questionable citations of Burchard manuscripts include: Bologna, Bibl. Com. dell' Archiginn. 2599 should be read as Bologna, Biblioteca Universitaria, 2599 (Cat. 1358; concerning this ms., Fransen notes: 'il faut supprimer [ce ms.] ... [c'est] abrégé ... ainsi que Olomouc 202 [*sic*])'; Freiburg i. Breisgau, Universitätsbibliothek, 7 is cited in the literature variously as 7 or 8; the correct shelfmark is 7; Caiazzo, Cap. Arch., or Bibl. Vatican, sine num. is now Vaticano, Città del, Biblioteca Apostolica Vaticana, Vat. lat. 14731; Chartres, Bibliothèque Municipale, 534 is an erroneous citation of Chartres, Bibliothèque Municipale, 234; Firenze, Biblioteca Nazionale Centrale, Conv. soppr. A.4.254 (saec. XIII; cf. G. Fransen, 'Trois notes: Note sur le MS Saint-Omer 107; Collections canoniques oubliées; Burchard de Worms: Quête des manuscrits,' *Traditio* 26 [1970] pp. 444-447, is not Burchard, but Brocard, O.P., saec. XIII); Firenze, Biblioteca Medicea Laurenziana, 7.1: see note for Bologna supra; Hereford, Cathedral Library, O.2.VII, sometimes cited as a Burchard manuscript, is actually a manuscript of the

Collectio 17 librorum; Montpellier, Bibliothèque Municipale, 7 is sometimes cited as Montpellier, Bibliothèque Universitaire, 7; Olomouc, Kapitulní Knihova, now in Státni vědecká knihovna, Univerzitní knihovna (olim Univerzita palackého), 202, sometimes cited as a Burchard manuscript, is described as containing material from the *Collectio 12 Partium*, mixed with Burchard material; Oxford, St. John's College, 125 (Ivo's *Panormia*); Paris, Bibliothèque Nationale, lat. 297-8 is a superseded shelfmark: see Paris B.N. lat. 11578; Paris, Bibliothèque Nationale, lat. 375 is a superseded shelfmark: see Paris B.N. lat. 12449; Paris, Bibliothèque Nationale, lat. 393 is a superseded shelfmark: see Paris B.N. lat. 9630; In correction of J. Rambaud Buhot, 'Baluze, bibliothécaire et canoniste' in *Études d'histoire du droit canonique dédiées à Gabriel Le Bras* (Paris, 1965) 1, p. 330, n. 32. Ms. Paris B.N. lat. 3683 should read 3863; Pistoia, Cap. C. 73 is not Burchard, but Brocard, O.P. (saec. XIII); Reims, Bibliothèque Municipale, 675 (G 528), sometimes cited as a Burchard manuscript, is actually a manuscript of the *Collectio 17 librorum*; St-Claude, Bibliothèque Municipale, 17 (*Cat. gén.* 3), sometimes cited as a Burchard manuscript, is actually a manuscript of the *Collectio 12 Partium;* Torino, Bibl. Comm., 150, citation false, but may refer to Ivrea, Biblioteca Capitolare, XCIV (50); Troyes, Bibliothèque Municipale, 246 (saec. XI; Troyes) cited in catalogue as Burchard, is actually a manuscript of the *Collectio 12 Partium;* Vaticano, Città del, Biblioteca Apostolica Vaticana, Vat. lat. 9201 does not contain Burchard; Vat. lat. 9522 does not contain Burchard; Vat. lat. 1450 (Burchard) should be read as Barb. lat. 1450; Vercelli, Biblioteca Capitolare, T.IV.214 is now Monza, Biblioteca Capitolare, H-5/154 (saec. XI); Wien, Österreichische Nationalbibliothek, lat. 354 (saec. XII; 1147x1164; Salzburg) is described as containing material from the *Collectio 12 Partium*, mixed with Burchard material; and lat. 2044 [fragment] has since 1923 been Napoli, Biblioteca Nazionale Vittorio Emanuele II, Cod. Vind. lat. 23.

B. Manuscripts of the *Diversorum patrum sententie sive Collectio in LXXIV titulos digesta* (see above, n. 8)

Angers, Bibliothèque Municipale, 278 (269) (saec. X; provenance St-Aubin) [excerpt from 74T in saec. XI hand, from *4 Books* redaction]; Berlin, Staatsbibliothek zu Berlin, Preussischer Kulturbesitz, Theol. lat. fol. 281 (saec. XII; Prüm); Bruxelles, Bibliothèque Royale Albert Ier, 9706-25 (Cat. 1360) (saec. XII^{in}; probably St-Laurent at Liège); El Escorial, Real Biblioteca de San Lorenzo, L.III.19 (saec. XI/XII; southern Italy, possibly Montecassino); and Z.III.19 (saec. XI^{ex}; southern Italy); Engelberg, Stiftsbibliothek, 52 (olim I 4/2) (saec. XI/XII; Swabian, possibly St. Blasien, later at

Engelberg); Firenze, Biblioteca Medicea Laurenziana, 16.15 (saec. XI/XII); and Conv. soppr. 91 [olim Badia 2685] (saec. XII^{in}; Italy, provenance Santa Maria e Benedetto in Albarese); Montecassino, Archivio dell'Abbazia, 522 (saec. XI/XII; probably Montecassino); München, Bayerische Staatsbibliothek, Clm. 9515 (saec. IX/X) [excerpt]; Clm. 22289 (saec. XII) [excerpt]; Namur, Musée Archéologique, 5 (saec. XI^{ex}; St-Hubert-en-Ardennes); New Haven, Yale University, Law Library, 31 (saec. XI/XII; Belgium or northeast France, probably St-Laurent at Liège); Roma, Biblioteca Casanatense, 2010 [olim B.V.17] (saec. XI^{ex}; possibly Rome); Roma, Biblioteca Vallicelliana, F 54 (saec. XI/XII; southern Italy); San Daniele del Friuli, Biblioteca Civica Guarneriana, 203 (saec. XII; Italy); Sankt Gallen, Stiftsbibliothek, 676 (saec. XI, ca. 1080 x 1100; St. Blasien or Schaffhausen, later at St. Gall); Stuttgart, Württembergische Landesbibliothek, HB.VI.107 (olim Weingarten C.6) (saec. XI^{ex}; probably Constance, St. Blasien, or Schaffhausen, later to Weingarten); and Cod. fragment 41 (saec. XI; Constance) [excerpt]; Vaticano, Città del, Biblioteca Apostolica Vaticana, Vat. lat. 4160 (saec. XI^{ex}; Italian); Vat. lat. 4977 (saec. XI-XII) [excerpt]; Reg. lat. 818 (a. 1536); Reg. lat. 1054 (Montfaucon 224; olim Petau D.117) (saec. XI; Pseudo-Isidore; excerpt from 74T in saec. XII hand); Wien, Österreichische Nationalbibliothek, lat. 2153 (Iur. Can. 38) (saec. XII^{in}; lower Austria or northern Italy, later at St. Pölten); and lat. 2206 (Salzburg 295) (saec. XII^{in}); Wolfenbüttel, Herzog-August-Bibliothek, 9.4.Aug.4° (Heinemann 2985) (saec. XII).

C. Manuscripts of the *Collectio canonum* of Anselm of Lucca (see above, n. 9)

Berlin, Staatsbibliothek zu Berlin, Preussischer Kulturbesitz, lat. fol. 597; Bologna, Biblioteca Universitaria, 375 (saec XII) [fragment] [Rec. B]; Cambridge, Corpus Christi College, 269 (saec. XII) [Rec. A]; Firenze, Biblioteca Medicea Laurenziana, Ashburnham 53 (saec. XII) [Rec. A2]; and San Marco 499 (saec. XII; middle Italian, Tuscany?) [Rec. A1]; Graz, Universitätsbibliothek, II.351 (saec. XII) [Rec. A1]; Huesca, Biblioteca Pública Provincial, 20 (saec. XVI) [Rec. C]; Leipzig, Universitätsbibliothek, Haenel 31 (3528) (19th c., G. Haenel; transcript of Paris 12450); Mantova, Biblioteca Comunale, C.II.23 (318) (saec XII^{in}) [Rec. A]; Milano, Biblioteca Ambrosiana, A.46.sup; and C.287.inf. (saec. XVI-XVII, ante a. 1619); Napoli, Biblioteca Nazionale Vittorio Emanuele II, XII.A.27; XII.A.37-39 (saec. XII) [Rec. A1]; Paris, Bibliothèque Nationale, lat. 1444 (saec. XVI); lat. 12450-51 (olim Sangerm. 939) (saec. XVII) = transcript of Vat. Lat. 4983 + Vat. Barb. lat. 535; lat. 12519 (saec. XII) [Rec. A2]; Parma, Bibliotheca

Nazionale Palatina, fondo Parmense 976 (saec. XII^{ex}; Italian) [Rec. A1]; Pisa, Biblioteca del Seminario Santa Caterina, 59 (56) (saec. XII) [Rec. A]; Vaticano, Città del, Biblioteca Apostolica Vaticana, Vat. lat. 1361 (saec. XII) [Rec. A]; Vat. lat. 1363 (saec. XII) [Rec. A2]; Vat. lat. 1364 (saec. XII^{in}) [Rec. B]; Vat. lat. 3531 (saec. XVI) [Rec. A]; Vat. lat. 3832 (saec. XI) ; Vat. lat. 4983 (saec. XVI) [Rec. C]; Vat. lat. 6381 (saec. XII) [Rec. B]; Barb. lat. 535 (olim Barb. XI.178) (saec. XII^{in}) [Rec. Bb]; Ottob. lat. 224 (a. 1600; transcript of Vat. lat. 4983) [Rec. C]; and Reg. lat. 325; Venezia, Biblioteca Nazionale Marciana, IV.LV (2243) (saec. XII) [Rec. A1].

D. Manuscripts of the unedited *Tripartita* of Ivo of Chartres (see above, n. 10)

Admont, Stiftsbibliothek 162 (saec. XII); Alençon, Bibliothèque Municipale, 135 (saec. XII); Berkeley, University of California Law Library, Robbins 102 (saec. XII^{in}); Berlin, Staatsbibliothek zu Berlin, lat. fol. 197 (saec. XII); and Hamilton 345 (saec. XIII; Italy); Brugge, Stedelijke Bibliotheek, 99 (saec. XII; provenance Ter Duinen); Burgo de Osma, Archivo Biblioteca de la Santa Iglesia Catedral (saec. XIII) ; Cambridge, Gonville and Caius College, 393 (455) (saec. XII); Cambridge, Jesus College, Q.G.4 (52) [prologue]; Gniezno, Archiwum Archidiecezjalne i Biblioteka kapitulna, 25 (saec. XII); Göttweig, Stiftsbibliothek, 56 (saec. XII) [extracts]; København, Kongelike Bibliotek, Thott. 555^{4o} (saec. XII); Kraków, Archiwum Kapituly Metropolitalnej Krakowskiej, 84 (a. 1099-1110); Lambach, Bibliothek des Benediktinerstifts, Cml. CVII (saec. XII) [incomplete]; Lincoln, Cathedral Library, 193 [extracts]; London, British Library, Cotton Cleopatra C.VIII (saec. XII) [extracts]; München, Bayerische Staatsbibliothek, Clm. 12603 (saec. XIII); and Clm. 17099; Olomouc, Kapitulní Knihova, now in Státni vědecké knihovna, Univerzitní knihovna (olim Univerzitní palackého), 205 (saec. XII); Oxford, Bodleian Library, d'Orville 46 (saec. XII); Paris, Bibliothèque Nationale, lat. 3858 (saec. XII; provenance Troyes); lat. 3858A (saec. XII); 3858B (saec. XII); lat. 4282 (saec. XII); lat. 13656 (saec. XII); Vaticano, Città del, Biblioteca Apostolica Vaticana, Reg. lat. 973 (saec. XII); Vorau, Stiftsbibliothek, 350 (saec. XII); Wien, Österreichische Nationalbibliothek, lat. 982 (Theol. 335) (saec. XII) [incomplete]; Wolfenbüttel, Herzog-August-Bibliothek, 180 (207) Helmst. (saec. XIII^{in}).

E. Manuscripts of the *Decretum* of Ivo of Chartres (see above, n. 11)

Cambridge, Corpus Christi College, 19 (saec. XII; Canterbury); Koblenz, Landeshauptarchiv, Best 701, Nr. 759.35 (saec. $XII^{1/2}$) [fragment]; Köln, lost manuscript (cf. P. Landau, 'Das Dekret des Ivo von Chartres: Die handschriftliche Überlieferung im Vergleich zum Text in den Editionen des 16. und 17. Jahrhunderts,' *Zeitschrift der Savigny-Stiftung für Rechtsgeschichte, Kanonistische Abteilung* 70 [1984] pp. 1-44, esp. 14-17, 27-30); Leiden, Bibliotheek van de Rijksuniversiteit, B.P.L. 184 [extracts]; Leipzig, Universitätsbibliothek, 955.4 [extracts]; London, British Library, Harley 3090 (saec. XII) [extracts]; and Royal 11.D.VII (saec. XII; provenance Lincoln); Paris, Bibliothèque de l'Arsenal, 713 (II.B.L.) (saec. XII^{ex}; provenance St-Victor); Paris, Bibliothèque Nationale, lat. 3874 (Colbert 935) (saec. XII); lat. 4809 (saec. XIII^{ex}) [extracts]; and lat. 14315 (saec. XII; provenance St-Victor); Roma, Biblioteca dell'Accademia Nazionale dei Lincei, Corsin. 1808 (saec. XII) [extracts]; Siguënza, Biblioteca del Cabildo, 61; Vaticano, Città del, Biblioteca Apostolica Vaticana, Vat. lat. 1357 (saec. XII-XIII; provenance France); and Pal. lat. 587 (saec. XII; Germany?); Wien, Österrichische Nationalbibliothek, lat. 2196 (789) (saec. XII) [extracts].

F. Manuscripts of the *Panormia* of Ivo of Chartres (see above, n. 12)

Admont, Stiftsbibliothek, 257 (saec. XII); and 541; Amiens, Bibliothèque Communale de la Ville, Fonds Lescalopier 10; Angers, Bibliothèque Municipale, 369; Avranches, Bibliothèque Municipale, 147; Bamberg, Staatsbibliothek, Can. 90; Berlin, Staatsbibliothek zu Berlin, lat. qu. 106; Preussischer Kulturbesitz, 613-614; Preussischer Kulturbesitz, Savigny 13; Bern, Burgerbibliothek, 422; Bruxelles, Bibliothèque Royale Albert Ier, 1817 (Cat. 2501) (saec. XII); Burgo de Osma, Archivo Biblioteca de la Santa Iglesia Catedral, 8, (saec. XIII; provenance France); Cambridge, Corpus Christi College, 94; Cambridge, Pembroke College, 103 (saec. XIII; England); Cambridge, University Library, Ff.IV.41 (saec. XIII); and Li.IV.28 (saec. XII^{ex}; England); Douai, Bibliothèque Municipale, 584; Einsiedeln, Stiftsbibliothek, 196; El Escorial, Real Biblioteca de San Lorenzo, d.III.14 (saec. XII) [prologue, excerpts]; Engelberg, Stiftsbibliothek, 56-57; Evreux, Bibliothèque Municipale, 25; Firenze, Biblioteca Medicea Laurenziana, San Marco 487; and San Marco 499; Firenze, Biblioteca Nazionale Centrale, Conv. soppr. G.I.836 (Vallombrosa); Gent, Centrale Bibliotheek van de Rijksuniversiteit, 553; and 2094; Graz, Universitätsbibliothek, 327; and 887; Hereford, Cathedral Library, O.6.XIII (saec. XII; Hereford); Klosterneuburg, Stiftsbibliothek, 638/1; Koblenz, Landeshauptarchiv, 701 Nr. 759,7; København, Kongelike Bibliotek, Thott 158 fol.; and Thott 555.4°; Kraków, Biblioteka Jagiellońska, 613; and 614; Lincoln, Cathedral Library, 192 (saec. XII); London, British Library, Arundel 252; Cotton Vitellius A.III (saec. XII); Egerton 749 (saec. XII); Royal 7.B.V (saec. XIII); Royal 10.A.VIII; Royal 11.B.XIII; Add. 11440 (saec. XII) [excerpts]; Add. 17513;

Add. 18371 (saec. XIII; provenance St. Georgenberg) [abridgement]; and Add. 22802 (saec. XII) [excerpts]; Luxembourg, Bibliothèque Nationale, 49; Madrid, Biblioteca Nacional, R 127; Mantova, Biblioteca Comunale, 198 (B.II.21); Marburg, Hessisches Staatsarchiv, Hr. 9 Fasc. 4 (saec. XIII) [fragment]; Modena, Biblioteca Estense, XII.F.28; Montecassino, Archivio dell' Abbazia, 215 Z; München, Bayerische Staatsbibliothek, Clm. 2593 (provenance Aldersbach); Clm. 4545 (saec. XII/XIII; provenance Benediktbeuern); Clm. 6354 (provenance Freising); Clm. 11316 (provenance Polling); Clm. 17099 (provenance Schäftlarn); Clm. 17100 (Schäftlarn); Clm. 22289 (provenance Windberg) [extracts]; Clm. 28223 (saec. XIII; Karlsheim); and Clm. 29172 (St. Mang); Napoli, Societá Patria Cuomo MS 1-5-14 (saec. XIII) [excerpts]; Orléans, Bibliothèque Municipale, 222 (194) (saec. XII; provenance Fleury); Oxford, Bodleian Library, Bodley 388 (saec. XII); Laud. 226; Laud. misc. 547 (saec. XII); and Lyell 40 (excerpt); Oxford, Jesus College, 26 (saec. XII); and 50 (saec. XII^{in}); Oxford, St. John's College, 125 (saec. XII); Paris, Bibliothèque de l'Arsenal, 713 (II.B.L.) (saec. XII^{ex}; provenance St.-Victor); Paris, Bibliothèque Mazarine, 1286 (1203); Paris, Bibliothèque Nationale, lat. 1359 (saec. XIII); lat. 2472 (saec. XII); lat. 2703 (saec. XII); lat. 3348 (saec. XII$^{2/2}$); lat. 3864; lat. 3865; lat. 3866; lat. 3867; lat. 3868; lat. 3869; lat. 3869A; lat. 3870; lat. 3871; lat. 3872; lat. 3873; lat. 4284; lat. 4285; lat. 7710; lat. 10742 (saec. XII); lat. 13660 (saec. XII); lat. 14135 [fragment]; lat. 14145 (saec. XII); lat. 14994 (saec. XII); lat. 14995 (saec. XII); lat. 17526 (saec. XII); and lat. 18222 (saec. XII); Parma, Biblioteca Nazionale Palatina, V.22; and 680; Philadelphia, University of Pennsylvania Library, 58; Roma, Biblioteca Nazionale Centrale Vittorio Emanuele II, 2086 (Sess. 64); Roma, Biblioteca dell'Accademia Nazionale dei Lincei, Corsin. 1365; Rouen, Bibliothèque Municipale, A.330 (705) (saec. XII; St-Evroul); St-Omer, Bibliothèque Municipale, 360; 364; and 381; Salzburg, Stiftsbibliothek Sankt Peter, a.VIII.15 (saec. XII); Siguënza, Biblioteca del Cabildo, 5 mod. (207) (saec. XII); and 75 mod. (160) (saec. XII-XIII); Sankt Gallen, Stiftsbibliothek, 620 [prologue]; Sankt Paul im Lavanttal, Stiftsbibliothek, 22/1 (saec. XII); St. Petersburg, Rossiyskaya Natsional'naya Biblioteka, O.v.II.4 (saec. XII-XIII); and Erm. lat. 25 (saec. XII); Strasbourg, Bibliothèque municipale, 108; Torino, Biblioteca Nazionale Universitaria, D.V.19 (saec. XII) [excerpt]; and E.V.16 (saec. XIII); Trier, Stadtbibliothek, 909; and 910/1114 (saec. XII); Troyes, Bibliothèque Municipale, 480 (saec. XII$^{2/4}$; Library of Bernard of Clairvaux); 1293; 1328; and 1519; Utrecht, Bibliotheek van de Rijksuniversiteit, 621 (saec. XIII/XIV); Vaticano, Città del, Biblioteca Apostolica Vaticana, Vat. lat. 1358; Vat. lat. 1359; Vat. lat. 1360; Vat. lat. 1362 (provenance Santa Maria in Crescenazgo, Milan); Vat. lat. 1363; Vat. lat. 5002; Arch. San Pietro G.19 (saec. XII$^{3/4}$; France); Arch. San Pietro G.19bis (saec. XII); Barb. lat. 502; Barb. lat. 534; Ottob. lat. 164; Reg. lat. 340; Reg. lat. 972; Reg.

lat. 991; and Reg. lat. 992; Vendôme, Bibliothèque Municipale, 160; Venezia, Biblioteca Nazionale Marciana, San Marco 12; Vic, Archivo Capitular, 95; and 145; Wien, Österreichische Nationalbibliothek, lat. 986; lat. 2192 (saec. XII); lat. 2200; lat. 2212; and lat. 5130; Zwettl, Stiftsbibliothek, 231.

Collectio canonum Casinensis duodecim saeculi

Montecassino, Archivio dell'Abbazia, MS 216

p. 1 ⟨I⟩ INSTITUTIO SANCTORUM PATRUM DE QUALITATE CULPARUM ET DE DISCIPLINA ATQUE DOCTRINA SACERDOTUM.

p. 4 Institutio illa sancta que fiebat in diebus ... / ... dictis et sententiis ista omnia describimus.

(5L 4.49, C. p. 209, and Burchard 19.8, PL 140.978, MC 45, p. 355, MC 44, p. 263)

⟨II⟩ QUOD NULLI SACERDOTUM CANONES LICEAT IGNORARE.

EX DICTIS CELESTINI PAPA (*sic*).

Nulli sacerdotum liceat suos canones ignorare ... aliquorum libitu licentia populis permissa frangantur.

(5L 2.1 Forn. 179, C. p. 67; and cf. Burchard. 2.160, PL 140.652, and MC 1, p. 218 and MC 439, p. 206)

⟨III⟩ UT SACERDOTES DILIGENTER EXAMINENT CONFITENTIUM PECCATA.

Episcopi et presbiteri examinent qualiter confitentium peccata diiudicent et tempus penitentie constituant.

(Burchard 19.98, PL 140.1003, MC 45, p. 324, MC 44, p. 276)

Nulli quoque penitentiam ex corde suo sed auctoritate sacrorum canonum iniungant.

(fons non invenitur)

p. 5 ⟨IV⟩ UT SINGULI PRESBITERI CAPITULA CANONUM HABEANT / AD SUCURRENDUM PENITENTIBUS.

EX CONCILIO MOGATIENSIS.

Unusquisque presbiter capitula habeant de maioribus ... subditis ut caveant ab insidiis diaboli.

(Burchard 19.99, PL 140.1003, MC 45, p. 324, MC 44, p. 276)

⟨V⟩ DE PRESBITERIS QUI CULPAS PECCANTIUM RETICENT VEL MINUS DIGNE PENITENTES AD RECONCILIATIONEM ADDUCUNT.

EX DECRETIS ALEXANDRI PAPE.

p. 6 Nemo presbiterorum xenium vel quodcumque emolumentum ... / ... et deo et hominibus contrarium est.

(Burchard 19.100, PL 140.1003, MC 45, p. 324, MC 44, p. 276)

⟨VI⟩ NE PECCATORUM CONFESSIONEM PALAM RECITETUR.

Leo episcopus. Non est publice confitendum peccatum sed absconse ... quia precator eius fiat ad deum.

(5L 4.41a, C. p. 206)

⟨VII⟩ DE EODEM.

GREGORII DICTA.

p. 7 Caveat ante omnia sacerdos ne de ius ... / ... omnibus diebus vite sue ignominiosus peregrinando peniteat.

(5L 4.41b[2], C. p. 207)

⟨VIII⟩ QUOD NON OPORTEAT MANIFESTAM CULPAM OCCULTE CORRIGI.

SMARAGDUS.

Manifesta peccata non sunt occulta correctione ... quam per unius licentiam multi periclitentur.

(5L 4.45, C. p. 207)

⟨IX⟩ UT NULLUS EPISCOPUS SEU PRESBITER ALTERIUS PENITENTEM SINE LITTERIS SUI EPISCOPI SUSCIPIAT.

EX EPISTOLA FELICIS PAPE.

p. 8 Curandum vero maxime et omni cautela ... / ... in quibus hoc minus curatum fuerit commorantur.

(5L 4.34c, C. p. 204; and cf. Burchard 19.62, PL 140.998, MC 45, p. 370, MC 44, p. 274)

⟨X⟩ UT PENITENTIA NULLI NEGETUR POSITO IN ULTIMIS.

Gregorius. Si quis penitentiam alicui in periculo posito abnegaverit funditus degradetur.

(5L 4.33b, C. p. 204)

⟨XI⟩ UT PENITENTIA TEMPORA IUXTA QUALITATEM PECCATI DECERNANTUR.

EX CONCILIO AFRICANO.

Penitentibus secundum differentiam peccatorum sacerdotis arbitrio penitentie tempora decernantur.

(cf. 5L 4.34, C. p. 204)

⟨XII⟩ QUE PENITENTIA MELIOR SIT.

SYNODUS ROMANA.

Melior est penitentia brevis cum fervore ... remissa in qua nichil districte
p. 9 cogitur. /

(cf. 5L 4.7c, C. p. 190)

⟨XIII⟩ DE ILLIS QUI DE GRADU ECCLESIASTICO ALIQUOS OCCIDERINT.

Synodus Nicena. Qui episcopum occiderit secundum antiquam diffinitionem ... residuos septem ut supradictum est penitentia.

(cf. 5L 4.63c, C. p. 215)

⟨XIV⟩ De homicidio clericorum.

Iudicium Commeani.

p. 10 Si quis episcopus homicidium fecerit xv. ... / ... corporis recipiat quanto magis ordines clericorum.

(cf. 5L 4.64, C. p. 215)

⟨XV⟩ De homicidio in ecclesia vel in atrio eius.

Ex concilio Calcedonensis.

p. 11 Si quis homicidium in ecclesia aut ... / ... et flendo dignam demonstraverit habere penitentiam.

(fons non invenitur)

⟨XVI⟩ De diversis homicidiis voluntariis sive non voluntariis.

Sancta synodus cl. patrum sub Theodosio seniore Constantinopolim congregata pro plerosque simplices minusque capaces hoc strictim breviter
p. 14 que ... / ... diaconus etiam xii., episcopus xv. et cetera similiter.

(cf. 5L 4.79, C. p. 218)

⟨XVII⟩ De homicidio laycorum.

Si quis laicus alterum laicum pro rixas ... iussionem domini sui xl. dies penitentia.

(cf. 5L 4.71b, C. p. 217)

⟨XVIII⟩ De septem generibus nolentium homicidiorum.

Ex concilio Constantinopolitano.

p. 17 Sex genera sunt nolentia homocidiorum primum ... / ... tamen difficile sine neglegentia hoc invenitur.

(cf. 5L 4.80, C. p. 219)

⟨XIX⟩ Ex decretis Silvestri pape.

Si quis homines publice penitentem interfecerit ... et nisi in finem non communicet.

(cf. Burchard 6.20, PL 140.769, MC 45, p. 198, MC 44, p. 152)

⟨XX⟩ Ex concilio Mogatiensi.

Qui odii meditatione vel propter cupiditatem ... xl. dies penitentiam in pane et aqua.

(Burchard 6.33, PL 140.772, MC 45, p. 200, MC 44, p. 154)

⟨XXI⟩ De illo qui servum suum interfecerit.

Ex concilio Agathensis.

Si quis servum proprium sine conscientia ... occiderit ut homicidium
p.18 sponte commissum iugeat. /

(Burchard 6.18, PL 140.769, MC 45, p. 198, MC 44, p.152; and cf. 5L 4.68, C. p. 216)

⟨XXII⟩ De servo qui dominum suum interfecerit.

Synodus Hybernensis.

Si quis servus dominum suum voluntarie occiderit ... si autem nolens septem anni remissuis (*sic*) penitentia.

(5L 4.67, C. p. 216)

⟨XXIII⟩ De domina que ancillam suam adeo flagellat ut moriatur.

Ex concilio Heliberitano.

Si qua domina furore zeli accensa ... ista tempora constituta fuerit infirmata accipiat communionem.

(Burchard 6.19, PL 140.769, MC 45, p. 198, MC 44, p. 152; cf. MC 541, p. 254)

⟨XXIV⟩ DE HIS QUI SE IPSOS OCCIDERINT ET QUI PRO SUIS SCELERIBUS PUNIUN-
p. 19 TUR. /

Preceptum ynodale precipue tamen Romanum. Si quis vexatur a demo-
p. 20 ne et nescit ... / ... perire quam per unum multos periclitari.

(5L 5.122u, C. p. 344)

⟨XXV⟩ EX CONCILIO AURELIANENSI.

p. 21 Si fur aut latro captus in preda ... / ... autem diebus vite sue penitentiam agat.

(Burchard 11.60, PL 140.870, MC 45, p. 276, MC 44, p. 203)

⟨XXVI⟩ IUDICIUM THEODORI.

Si quis ultimo ad spectaculum mortis ... qui est moriturus in tales xl. dies penitentia.

(fons non invenitur)

⟨XXVII⟩ IUDICIUM CANONUM.

p. 22 Si quis homicidium consenserit faciendum et factum ... / ... et non potuerit iii. anni peniteat.

Paenitentiale Vallicellianum I (Schmitz I.254)

⟨XXVIII⟩ IN CONCILII CANONUM.

p. 23 Si quis castrum sponte incenderit per multa ... / ... penitentiam dignam egerit communio ei tribuatur.

(fons non invenitur)

⟨XXIX⟩ EX PENITENTIALI ROMANO.

Si quis prebet ducatum barbaris tredecim annos peniteat ... ad mortem mundo mortuus deo vivat.

(Burchard 19.103, PL 140.1004, MC 45, p. 374, MC 44, p. 277; and 5L 3.341, Forn. 494, C. p. 183)

⟨XXX⟩ Ex concilio Heliberitano.

Si quis delator extiterit fidelis et ... et post tres annos accipere communionem.

(5L 4.92b, C. p. 222)

⟨XXXI⟩ De maleficio.

Synodus Ancirana.

p. 24 Si quis per maleficia aliquem hominem ... / ... tamen non affectauerit iii. anni penitentiam.

(5L 4.72a, C. p. 217)

⟨XXXII⟩ Ex concilio Heliberitano.

Si quis per qualecumque maleficium interfecit ... communionem nisi cum satisfactionibus digne emendaverit.

(5L 4.72b, C. p. 217)

⟨XXXIII⟩ De proditoribus.

Synodus Romana.

p. 25 Si quis castellum aut alicuius municipium ... / ... luctu iuxta vires suas iugiter penitentiam.

(cf. 5L 4.182, C. p. 220)

⟨XXXIV⟩ De eo qui hominem captivaverat.

Si quis servum aut quecumque hominem ... potuerit et noluerit ut impius iudicetur.

(5L 4.136, C. p. 235)

⟨XXXV⟩ DE PERCUSSORIBUS.

Si quis alium per iram percusserit ... episcopus ii. annos et sex mensibus.

(Burchard 19.119, PL 140.1007 [not in MC 45 or MC 44]; and cf. 5L 4.153i, C. p. 243)

p. 26 ⟨XXXVI⟩ ITEM. /

Fecisti truncationem manuum aut pedum aut oculos ... in pane et aqua penitere debes.

(Burchard 19.5, PL 140.955, MC 45, p. 339, MC 44, p. 250)

⟨XXXVII⟩ ITEM.

p. 27 Qui per rixam et ictum debilem ... / ... xl. dies peniteat in pane et aqua.

(Burchard 19.101, PL 140.1004, MC 45, p. 374, MC 44, p. 277; cf. 5L, 4.154, C. p. 244)

⟨XXXVIII⟩ ITEM.

Si quis super patrem suum vel matrem ... vel patre vel matre in Christo.

(fons non invenitur)

⟨XXXIX⟩ DE VIRO QUI UXOREM SUAM CUM CAUSALE SINE CAUSA OCCIDERIT AUT MULIER VIRUM SUUM.

Placuit sancto et magno Calcedonensi concilio dcxxx. sacerdotes sub
p. 28 Marciano principe affuerunt ut si quis vir uxorem ... / ... non nisi ad
mortem exitum percipiat.

(5L 4.81, C. p. 219)

⟨XL⟩ DE PATRE VEL MATRE SI FILIUM SUUM NECAVERIT.

IUDICIUM CANONUM.

p. 29 Si pater scienter et voluntarie necat ... / ... modum culpe provideantur et vires hominis.

(5L 4.87, C. p. 221)

⟨XLI⟩ CONCILIO HELIBERITANO.

Si mater filium suum sponte occiderit ... propter difficultatem nutriendi septem anni peniteat.

(Burchard 19.156, PL 140.1013 [not in MC 45 or MC 44])

⟨XLII⟩ IUDICIUM COMMEANI.

Si qua mulier invenerit iuxta se ... iii. anni peniteat, si autem baptizatus duo.

(5L 4.84c, C. p. 220)

p. 30 Si qua mulier posuerit infantem suum ... / ... sua ii. anni peniteat, si vero baptizatus unum.

(5L 4.84b, C. p. 220)

⟨XLIII⟩ CAPITULUM EIUSDEM.

Si mulier se vivum vel sanum ... si vero baptizatus duas quadragesimas peniteat.

(5L 4.84c, C. p. 220)

⟨XLIV⟩ GREGORIUS.

Si qua fidelis mulier oppresserit per neglegentiam ... circa neglectum t(s)uum iudicio sacerdotis peniteat.

(5L 4.84a, C. p. 220)

⟨XLV⟩ Ex concilio Anciramo.

p. 31 Si quis conceptum mulieris deceperit si ... / ... post xl. dies ut homicidium peniteat.

(5L 4.87a, C. p. 221)

⟨XLVI⟩ Ex eodem concilio Anciramo.

Si qua mulier fornicaverit et infantem ... ipsarum decem annos agere peniteat iudicamus.

(5L 4.86, C. p. 221)

⟨XLVII⟩ Ex eodem concilio.

Posuisti infantem tuum iuxta ignem et alius ... aquam in caldariam misit innocens erit.

(Burchard 19.5, PL 140.974, MC 45, p. 352, MC 44, p. 261)

p. 32 ⟨XLVIII⟩ De feminis partus suos necantibus. /

Augustinus. Mulier que aut laborat ut non concipiat ... peccatum fuerit x. anni districte peniteat.

(5L 4.85c, C. p. 220)

⟨XLIX⟩ Item.

Nulla mulier potionem accipiat ut non concipiat ... esse cum patricidas causam reddituram.

(5L 4.85c, C. p. 221)

⟨L⟩ ITEM.

Nullas potiones diabolicas debent mulieres accipere ... debuerit tantorum homicidiorum ream esse cognoverit.

(5L 4.85c, C. p. 221)

⟨LI⟩ DE NUTRIENDIS AE PROCURANDIS FILIIS.

p. 33 SYNODUS HIBERNENSIS. /

Quicumque filios procreaverit causa pesteritatis nutrire ... enim scriptura carnem tuam ne despexeris.

(5L 4.108, C. p. 228)

⟨LII⟩ IERONIMUS.

Quicumque operator fuerit carnalis copule nutriendi ... fieri debet sin autem quiescat.

(5L 4.109, C. p. 228)

⟨LIII⟩ DE HIS QUI SE ABSCIDUNT.

IUDICIUM CANONUM.

Si quis quolibet membrum precipue tamen virilia ... laicus fuerit iii. anni excommunicationis peniteat.

(5L 4.89a, C. p. 222)

p. 34 ⟨LIV⟩ EX CONCILIO NICENO. /

Si quis a medicis per languorem ... et deinceps nullum debere talium promoveri.

(5L 1.139, Forn. 97, C. p. 41)

⟨LV⟩ DE DIVERSIS POLLUTIONIBUS.

IUDICIUM COMMEANI.

Si per cogitationem semen episcopus effuderit ... usque dum superetur talis violenta cogitatio.

(5L 5.98, C. p. 316)

⟨LVI⟩ IPSIUS.

p. 35 Qui per turpiloquium illud apostoli preceptum ... / ... iuxta gradus vel qualitatem peccati peniteat.

(5L 5.98, C. p. 316)

Si quis in nocte cogitaverit fantasias ... lavetur et communione ipsa die privetur.

(5L 5.98, C. p. 316)

Si quis sacerdos sine cogitatione pollutus ... ad sacrum officium si necesse fuerit accedat.

(5L 5.98, C. p. 316)

⟨LVII⟩ EX PENITENTIALI BEDE.

p. 36 Qui per illecebroso amplexus femine vel osculo ... / ... non fuerit pollutus viginti quattuor psalmos canet.

(Burchard 17.42, PL 140.927, MC 45, p. 319, MC 44, p. 235)

⟨LVIII⟩ EX PENITENTIALI ROMANO.

Clericus si semen fuderit non tangendo ... si presbiter xl. dies, si episcopus l. dies peniteat.

(Burchard 17.43, PL 140.928, MC 45, p. 319, MC 44, p. 236)

⟨LIX⟩ EX LIBRO QUI CORRECTOR VOCATUR.

Fecisti solus tecum fornicationes(m) ut quidam ... xx. dies in pane et aqua penitere debes.

(Burchard 19.5, PL 140.968, MC 45, p. 348, MC 44, p. 257)

⟨LX⟩ EX EODEM.

p. 37 Fecisti fornicationem ut quidam facere / solent ut tuum virile membrum ... si fecisti xx. dies in pane et aqua.

(Burchard 19.5, PL 140.968, MC 45, p. 348, MC 44, p. 257)

⟨LXI⟩ ITEM.

Fecisti fornicationem ut quidam facere solent ita dico ... xxx. dies in pane et. aqua. peniteas.

(Burchard 19.5, PL 140.968, MC 45, p. 348, MC 44, p. 257)

⟨LXII⟩ ITEM.

Si cum masculo inter coxas ut quidam ... xl. dies in pane et aqua peniteas.

(Burchard 19.5, PL. 140.968, MC 45, p. 348, MC 44, p. 257)

⟨LXIII⟩ DE VITIO SODOMITICUM.

p. 38 GREGORIUS. /

p. 39 Pueri qui fornicationem inter semetipsos iudicium ... / ... moris est suam compleat voluntatem iii. annos peniteat.

(5L 5.94b, C. p. 314, attributed to Iudicium Commeani)

⟨LXIV⟩ EX CONCILIO HILARDENSI.

De his qui se incesti pollutionem ... ad missam tantum cathecuminorum in ecclesia admittantur.

(Burchard 7.3, PL 140.780, MC 45, p. 206, MC 44, p. 158)

⟨LXV⟩ Ex penitentiali Romano.

p. 40 Viri inter femora fornicans unum annum ... / ... puer quindecim annos xl. dies peniteat.

(Excarpsus Cummeani 2.5-7, Schmitz 1.619)

⟨LXVI⟩ De sodomitis.

Gregorius.

p. 41 Si quis ordinatus in scelere sodomitico ... / ... congrua penitentia insuper verberibus afficiantur.

(5L 5.93c, C. p. 314)

⟨LXVII⟩ Iudicium Theodori.

Si quis per semetipsum quacumque ingenio fornicaverit ... circa quantitatem fornicationis et communionem privetur.

(5L 5.95a, C. p. 315)

⟨LXVIII⟩ Iudicium Commeani.

p. 42 Si quis fornicatio ut sodomite fecerit ... / ... si autem bene egerint penitentiam, reconcilientur ad communionem.

(5L 5. 94b, C. p. 314)

⟨LXIX⟩ Commeanus.

Si quis vir cum uxore sua retro nupserit ... si autem in terga penitentia sicut de animalibus.

(5L 5.86b, C. p. 312)

⟨LXX⟩ THEODORUS.

Mulier quocumque molimine aut in se ... cum altera fornicans ii. annos peniteat.

(Burchard 17.27, PL 140.924, MC 45, p. 316, MC 44, p. 233)

⟨LXXI⟩ IDEM IPSE.

Si sanctimonialis cum alia sanctimonialis per aliquod machinamentum
p. 43 fornicate fuerint vi. annos peniteat. /

(Burchard 17.28, PL 140.924, MC 45, p. 316, MC 44, p. 233)

⟨LXXII⟩ EX CONCILIO ANQUIRENSI.

Mulier si cum muliere fornicata fuerit ... inde plus eius accipiat amorem peniteat.

(Burchard 17.29, PL 140.924, MC 45, p. 316, MC 44, p. 233)

⟨LXXIII⟩ EX CONCILIO ANCIRANO, CAP. XV.

p. 44 De his qui irrationabiliter versati sunt ... / ... ad exitum vite communionis gratiam consequantur.

(5L 5.98a, C. p. 316; and Burchard 17.30, PL 140.924; MC 45, p. 316, MC 44, p. 234)

⟨LXXIV⟩ IUDICIUM THEODORI.

Animalia coytu hominum polluta occidantur carnesque ... ubi autem dubium est non occidantur.

(5L 5.98b, C. p. 316)

⟨LXXV⟩ IUDICIUM COMMEANI.

p. 45 Si osculatus est episcopus per desiderium ... / ... subdiaconus xx., clericus et laicus decem.

(5L 2.66.1, Forn. 218, C. p. 85)

⟨LXXVI⟩ SEQUITUR.

p. 46 Si semen per osculum fuderit episcopus iiii. annos peniteat ... / ... monachus x., clericus et laicus v. si sua non est.

(5L 2.66.2,3,4, Forn. 218, C. p. 85)

⟨LXXVII⟩ SEQUITUR.

Si semen per osculum fuderit episcopus i. annum peniteat ... ac ludibrius videtur osculum sacerdotis muliebricum.

(5L 2.66.5,6,7, Forn. 219, C. p. 85)

⟨LXXVIII⟩ EX CONCILIO AGATENSI.

p. 47 Si quis in ecclesia fornicatur quod nimis ... / ... subdiaconus i., clericus et laicus dimidium.

(5L 2.78.2, Forn. 227, C. p. 86)

⟨LXXIX⟩ IUDICIUM COMMEANI.

Si quis laicus non habens uxorem ... quod absit affectaverit septem annos peniteat.

(5L 5.74b, C. p. 306)

⟨LXXX⟩ DE ILLICITIS CONIUGIIS.

EX CONCILIO NICENO.

p. 48 Si quis duxerit de propria cogitatione ... / ... sive minus iuxta prolixiorem perpetrationem peccati.

(5L 5.110b, C. p. 329)

⟨LXXXI⟩ De diversis commixtionibus.

Synodus Calcedonensis dc xxx. sacerdotum sub Marciano principe habi-
p. 52 ta. Propter plerosque simplex ... / ... presbiter xv., episcopus xviii. annos. peniteat.

(5L 5.113b, C. p. 330)

⟨LXXXII⟩ De eo qui cum commatre vel matre aut filia in Christo fornicavit.

p. 53 Synodus Romana statuit, qui cum sua commatre ... / ... peccaverit ut congruum est mulieri condicioni.

(5L 5.114, C. p. 334)

⟨LXXXIII⟩ Ex concilio Mogatiensis.

p. 55 Si quis fornicatus fuerit cum duabus sororibus ... / ... avaritiam hominem occidunt quod morchidum vocant.

(Burchard 17.8, PL 140.920, MC 45, p. 313, MC 44, p. 231)

⟨LXXXIV⟩ Iudicium Commeani.

Molles id es (*sic*) effeminati qui super se feminas ... magnis vigiliis et orationibus et cautela discipline.

(fons non invenitur)

⟨LXXXV⟩ De facili fornicatione.

Gregorius.

p. 56 Si quis pontifex faciens facilem fornicationem ... / ... post actam penitentie reconcilietur ad communionem.

(5L 2.64 Forn. 217, C. p. 84)

⟨LXXXVI⟩ Ex concilio Medelsi (*sic*).

Si laicus cum femina laica, id est uterque ... et tempus addatur et modus penitentie.

(Burchard 9.68, PL 140.826, MC 45, p. 241, MC 44, p. 180)

⟨LXXXVII⟩ Ex concilio Mogatiensis.

p. 57 Si conscio marito et ipsa consentiente ... post annos decem ac/cipiat communionem.

(Burchard 9.69 PL 140.826, MC 45, p. 241, MC 44, p. 180)

⟨LXXXVIII⟩ Ex concilio Namtensis.

Quod si vir non habens uxorem ... libidinis impellente in fornicationem ceciderunt.

(Burchard 9.70, PL 140.827, MC 45, p. 241, MC 44, p. 180)

⟨LXXXIX⟩ De pluribus nuptiis.

Ex concilio Laodicensis.

Qui venerit in secundas nuptias penitentia ... si autem quintam difficile apta penitentia invenitur.

(5L 5.23, C. p. 277)

p. 58 ⟨XC⟩ Ex concilio neocesariensis. /

Si quis concupiscens fornicari etiamsi eius ... in qua fornicatus sunt ita peniteat.

(5L 2.67.1, Forn. 220, C. p. 86)

⟨XCI⟩ Iudicium Commeani.

p. 59 Si quis clericus aut monachus postquam deo se voverit ... / ... tale scelus commiserit pari sententia subiacebit.

(5L 2.134, Forn. 266, C. p. 106)

⟨XCII⟩ ITEM.

Si quis vir aut si qua mulier votum ... stulta vota fragenda sunt et importabilia.

(5L 2.134, Forn. 266, C. p. 106)

⟨XCIII⟩ EX CONCILIO HELIBERITANO.

Qui in quadragesima ante pascha cognoverit ... si non consuetudine occiderit xl. dies peniteat.

(Burchard 19.75, PL 140.1000, MC 45, p. 371, MC 44, p. 275)

⟨XCIV⟩ EX DECRETIS SANCTORUM PATRUM CONCILIORUM.

p. 60 Si quis episcopus, presbiter, diaconus etiam monachus qui / uxorem habuit ... obedire noluerint ecclesiam et communionem priventur.

(5L 2.58, Forn. 214, C. p. 83)

⟨XCV⟩ IUDICIUM COMMEANI.

p. 61 Si quis cum filia spirituali et ipsa ... / ... vel diacono tale scelus vel vitium commiserit.

(5L 2.79.2, Forn. 227, C. p. 86)

⟨XCVI⟩ IUDICIUM COMMEANI.

Si quis cum deo sacrata vel uxore ... et ad sacerdotii gradus nunquam accedant.

(5L 2.65, Forn. 218, C. p. 85)

p. 62 ⟨XCVII⟩ EX EPISTULA / HORMISDE PAPE ET EUGENII PAPE.

p. 63 Si qua femina in fornicatione deprehensa ... / ... possit et ignominiosa huius semper consistat.

(5L 2.75, Forn. 223, C. p. 88)

Si quis cum ea quam propter deum ... laicus vii. ex his in pane et aqua.

(5L 2.77, Forn. 225, C. p. 89)

⟨XCVIII⟩ DE EO QUI CUM SPONSA ALTERIUS FORNICAVERIT.

GREGORIUS.

Si quis cum sponsa alterius fornicaverit ... sacerdos gradus non presumant unquam accedere.

(5L 5.18, C. p. 275)

⟨XCIX⟩ EX CONCILIO BRACARENSI.

p. 64 Si devota peccaverit vel se marita/verit ... accedat, corruptorem etiam par pena constringat.

(5L 2.165, Forn. 279, C. p. 110)

⟨C⟩ IUDICIUM COMMEANI.

Si libera mulier publicum servum sibi copulaverit ... servo quam liber cum ancilla patiatur.

(5L 5.101, C. p. 319)

⟨CI⟩ ITEM DE EODEM.

p. 65 Si quis menstruo tempore coierit cum muliere ... / ... ante quadragesimam qui nupserit xx. dies peniteat.

(5L 5.85, C. p. 311)

Concubuisti cum uxore tua die dominico iiii. dies penitere debes.

(Burchard 19.5, PL 140.960, MC 45, p. 342, MC 44, p. 253)

Corrupisti virginem et postea eadem dixisti ... post corruptionem uxorem iii. annos peniteas.

(Burchard. 19.5, PL 140.958, MC 45, p. 341, MC 44, p. 252)

Si quis fidelis habens uxorem cum Iudea vel gentili ... poterit dominice communioni sociari.

(Ivo, Dec. 8.282, PL 161.645; Burchard 9.67, PL 140.826; cf. MC 554, p. 42; MC 541, pp. 179, 249)

⟨CII⟩ IOHANNES CHRISOSTOMUS.

p. 67 Si quis quod est mercatus incestuosissimum ... / ... criminis et conversationem simul et emendationem.

(5L 5.81, C. p. 309)

⟨CIII⟩ EX CONCILIO ANCIRANO.

Si qua puella desponsata alterius et postea rapta ... quidem consenserit raptori et corrupta fuerit.

(cf. MC 522, p. 264)

⟨CIV⟩ EX CONCILIO CALCEDONENSI.

Qui rapiunt puellas aut mulieres auctores ... raptas sibi iure coniungere nullatenus presumant.

(Burchard 9.36, PL 140.820, MC 45, p. 236, MC 44, p. 177; and cf. 5L 5.14b, C. p. 274)

⟨CV⟩ IUDICIUM PAPE LEONIS.

p. 68 Si quis acceperit eius qui captivatus est ... / ... ducta est eo quod inscii fecerunt.

(5L 5.68, C. p. 305)

⟨CVI⟩ EIUSDEM LEONIS PAPE.

Si qua mulier posteri viri amore capto ... emendaverit et tunc demum v. annos peniteat.

(5L 5.69, C. p. 305)

⟨CVII⟩ IOHANNES CHRISOSTOMUS, THEODORI, ET COMMEANI.

p. 69 Si quis uxorem suam invenerit adulteratam ... / ... invenerit adulterum non ad imparia iudicantur.

(5L 5.75, C. p. 307)

⟨CVIII⟩ BURCHARDUS IN LIBER (*sic*) QUI CORRECTOR VOCATUR.

Exercuisti lenocinium aut in te ipsa ... nisi in exitu non accipiat communionem.

(Burchard 19.5, PL 140.975, MC 45, p. 352, MC 44, p. 261)

Concubuisti cum uxore tua postquam infans ... vel saltum vel xl. dies
p. 70 ante partum decem dies peniteas. /

(cf. Burchard 19.5, PL 140.959, MC 45, p. 342, MC 44, p. 253)

Concubuisti cum uxore tua post manifestam conceptionem v. dies peniteas.

(cf. Burchard 19.5, PL 140.959, MC 45, p. 342, MC 44, p. 253)

⟨CIX⟩ DE MONACHO SI UXOREM ACCIPIAT.

SIRICIS PAPA.

Monachus si uxorem accipiat tantum in finem communicet similiter et monacha si maritum accipiat.

(5L 2.170, Forn. 281, C. p. 113)

⟨CX⟩ BURCHARDUS IN LIBER (*sic*) PREDICTO.

Mechatus es cum uxore alterius tu non habens uxorem ... carrina vocatur cum vii. sequentibus annis.

(Burchard 19.5, PL 140.957, MC 45, p. 341, MC 44, p. 251)

⟨CXI⟩ ITEM.

p. 72 Si mechatus es tu uxoratus cum alterius uxore ... / ... de uxore adulterium perpetrante dictum est.

(Burchard 19.5, PL 140.957, MC 45, p. 341, MC 44, p. 251)

⟨CXII⟩ EX CANONE APOSTOLORUM.

Si quis duas uxores habuerit aut uxorem ... accipiat nisi se alienaverit ex ea.

(fons non invenitur)

⟨CXIII⟩ IUDICIUM CANONUM.

Si quis laicus concubinam habere antequam uxorem ... vii. annos peniteat iuxta qualitatem vel quantitatem culpe.

(5L 5.27, C. p. 278)

⟨CXIV⟩ NE UXORES ACCIPERE HIS QUE SACROS ORDINES HABENT.

p. 73 Silvester episcopus. Nemo presbiter vel diaconus a die / ... si qua publice hoc egerit condempnetur imperpetuum.

(5L 2.72, Forn. 222) [not in C. There is a canon attributed to Sylvester in C. p. 87, but it is not the one used here]

⟨CXV⟩ EX CONCILIO NICENO.

Interdixit per omnia magna synodus non episcopo non presbitero ... quae a massculo (*sic*) subvenire non possit.

(5L 2.16, Forn. 189, C. p. 72; and Burchard 2.109, PL 140.645, MC 45, p. 85, MC 44, p. 77)

⟨CXVI⟩ Ex concilio Arelatensi.

Nullus episcopus, presbiter, diaconus aut subdiaconus ad secretum ... qui autem presumpserit canonice vindicte subiaceat.

(5L 2.19, Forn. 191, C. p. 73)

p. 74 ⟨CXVII⟩ Syricius papa ad Genesium episcopum /

Qui ordinatus episcopus aut presbiter aut ... episcopi quid de ea facere velit.

(5L 2.69, Forn. 221, C. p. 87)

⟨CXVIII⟩ In excerptis Martini pape.

Si quis episcopus, presbiter aut diaconus post diem ... ab ecclesia et inter laicos agat penitentiam.

(5L 2.71, Forn. 221, C. p. 87)

p. 75 ⟨CXIX⟩ Si monachus / filios genuerit.

Synodus statuit Romana: Monachi procreantes filios in carcere secludantur ... misericordie intuitu communionis possit gratia indulgeri.

(5L 2.171, Forn. 281, C. p. 113; and cf. Burchard 8.68; PL 140.806, MC 45, p. 226, MC 44, p. 170)

⟨CXX⟩ Ex decretis Zacharie pape et deusdedit.

Non oportet filiam de sacro fonte ... simul cum auctore sit ista condicio.

(5L 5.117b, C. p. 334)

⟨CXXI⟩ ITEM.

p. 76 Si quis cum scorta adulterium sepe ... / ... si se promiserit in antea emendaturam.

(fons non invenitur)

⟨CXXII⟩ EX CANONE APOSTOLORUM.

Presbiter aut diaconus qui in fornicatione ... scriptura, non iudicat dominus bis inidipsum.

(Burchard 2.189, PL 140.657, MC 45, p. 96, MC 44, p. 86)

⟨CXXIII⟩ DE PERIURIO.

IUDICIUM GREGORII PAPE.

p. 77 Si quis in altare ubi reliquie ... / ... tamen per consensum iii. annos peniteat.

(5L 4.143, C. p. 239)

⟨CXXIV⟩ EX PENITENTIALI THEODORI.

Qui periurat in manu episcopi aut in cruce ... et postea cognoscit iii. quadragesimas peniteat.

(Burchard 12.5, PL 140.877, MC 45, p. 281, MC 44, p. 206)

Honestum nobis et iustum videtur ... et pueri ante quattuordecim annos non cogatur iurare.

(Burchard 12.12, PL 140.878, MC 44, p. 207 [not in MC 45 because of lacuna in text])

⟨CXXV⟩ EX CONCILIO AURELIANENSIS.

Iuramentum filii aut filie nesciente parte ... nesciente abbate et iuramen-
p. 78 ta pueri irrita sunt. /

(Burchard 12.27, PL 140.831, attributed to Conc. Aurelianensis, MC 45, p. 283, MC 44, p. 208; and cf. 5L 4.139, C. p. 236, attributed to Synodus Hibernensis)

⟨CXXVI⟩ GREGORIUS.

Si quis invitus aut coactus qualibet causa ... necessitatis se periuraverit iii. annos peniteat.

(5L 4.145; C. p. 239, where invitus is a gloss on coactus)

⟨CXXVII⟩ EIUSDEM.

Si quis in manu episcopi vel presbiteri ... secundum antiquam diffinitionem v. annos peniteat.

(5L 4.146, C. p.239)

⟨CXXVIII⟩ EX PENITENTIALI ROMANO.

Si quis coactus pro vita redimenda ... iii. annos, unum ex his in pane et aqua.

(Burchard 12.6, PL 140.877, MC 45, p. 281, MC 44, p. 206)

⟨CXXIX⟩ EX LIBRO QUI DICITUR CORRECTOR.

p. 79 Fecisti periurium per cupiditatem xl. dies ... / ... monasterium ingressus iugi penitentia se subdat.

(Burchard 19.5, PL 140.956, MC 45, p. 340, MC 44, p. 251)

⟨CXXX⟩ EIUSDEM.

Fecisti periuriam sciens et alios in periurium ... si scientes fuerunt, sin autem levius.

(Burchard 19.5, PL 140.956, MC 45, p. 340, MC 44, p. 251)

⟨CXXXI⟩ DE EODEM.

Fecisti periurium coactus et per necessitatem ... in pane et aqua penitens et non redimas.

(Burchard. 19.5, PL 140.956, MC 45, p. 340, MC 44, p. 251)

⟨CXXXII⟩ EX DECRETIS PII PAPE.

p. 80 Qui compulsus a domino periurans se ... / ... eiusdem tres quadragesimas legitimas ferias peniteat.

(Burchard 12.4, PL 140.877, MC 45, p. 281, MC 44, p. 206)

⟨CXXXIII⟩ SYNODUS ROMANA.

Si quis inscius se periuraverit et postea ... ambo in laqueum diaboli strangulati sunt.

(5L 4.148b, C. p. 239)

⟨CXXXIV⟩ SYNODUS HIBERNENSIS.

Definitio incauta laudabiliter solvenda non prevaricatione sed temeritatis emendatio.

(5L 4.139, C. p. 236; and Burchard 12.25, PL 140.881, MC 45, p. 283, MC 44, p. 208)

⟨CXXXV⟩ EX DICTIS YSIDORI.

p. 81 Quacumque arte verborum quisque iuret deus ... / ... in vanum assumit et proximum dolo capit.

(5L 4.141b, C. p. 237)

⟨CXXXVI⟩ DE FALSO TESTIMONIO.

IUDICIUM COMMEANI.

Si quis falsum testimonium dixerit si episcopus ... clericus et laicus iii., unum ex his in pane et aqua.

(5L 4.94b, C. p. 223; and cf. MC 522, p. 192)

⟨CXXXVII⟩ ITEM.

Qui consenserit inscius ad falsum testimonium ... antequam studeas inquirat ii. annos peniteat.

(5L 4.94b, C. p. 223; and cf. MC 522, p. 192)

⟨CXXXVIII⟩ EX CONCILIO ARELATENSI.

Qui fratribus suis falso capitalia obiecisse ... ante constituit nisi digna satisfactione penituerint.

(Burchard 16.34, PL 140.917, MC 45, p. 311, MC 44, p. 229)

⟨CXXXIX⟩ EX CONCILIO CARTAGINENSIS.

p. 82 Si quis episcopum, presbiterum, vel diaconum aut aliquem / exordinatis falsis criminibus ... finem dandam ei non esse communionem.

(5L 4.92c, C. p. 223)

⟨CXL⟩ IN LIBRO QUI CORRECTOR DICITUR.

Fuisti in falso testimonio ita dico ... postea previde ne tibi ulterius contingat.

(Burchard 19.5, PL 140.960, MC 45, p. 343, MC 44, p. 253)

⟨CXLI⟩ DE TRACTORIBUS.

THEODORUS.

p. 83 Si quis episcopus alicui detrahit quindecim dies ... / ... diaconus et monachus decem, clerici et laici septem

(5L 4.145b, C. p. 244)

⟨CXLII⟩ DE ODIO.

Si quis hodio (*sic*) habens aliquem ita ... ab ecclesia dei separetur donec reconcilietur.

(Burchard 10.58, PL 140.852, MC 45, p. 263, MC 44, p. 193)

⟨CXLIII⟩ EX CONCILIO HILERDENSI.

Qui sacramento se obligaverit ut litiget ... que operit multitudinem peccatorum celeriter redeat.

(cf. 5L 4.149a, C. p. 240; and Burchard 12.17, PL 140.879, [MC 45, missing], MC 44, p. 208)

⟨CXLIV⟩ DE IRA.

IUDICIUM THEODORI ET COMMEANI.

Si quis contra alium iram tenet ... et aqua vivat usque dum reconcilietur ei.

(5L 4.144c, C. p. 244)

⟨CXLV⟩ ITEM.

p. 84 Si quis diu amaritudinem retinet in corde ... / ... pane et aqua cognoscat delictum suum.

(5L 4.144c, C. p. 244)

⟨CXLVI⟩ DE EODEM.

Qui verba acerbiora in furore non ... ruboreque tacuit unum diem peniteat in pane et aqua.

(5L 4.144c, C. p. 244)

⟨CXLVII⟩ DE EODEM.

Si quis commovetur et tantum sentit ... se conticuit quanto tempore contradixit tanto ieiunet.

(5L 4.144c, C. p. 244)

⟨CXLVIII⟩ DE EODEM.

p. 85 Si quis fratrem contristat iuste vel iniuste ... / ... cui maledixit placeat et septem dies in pane et aqua peniteat.

(5L 4.144c, C. p. 244)

⟨CXLIX⟩ DE MENDACIO.

IERONIMUS ET PATERIUS.

Si quis mendacium fecerit per ignorantiam ... iuxta nocituram providentia sacerdotis peniteat.

(5L 4.98a, C. p. 224)

⟨CL⟩ DE SACRILEGIO.

p. 86 EX DICTIS GREGORII PAPE. /

Sacrilegium id est sacrorum rerum furtum ... diaconus et monachus vii., subdiaconus v., clericus et laicus iiii.

(5L 4.124c, C. p. 233)

⟨CLI⟩ EX CONCILIO MOGATIENSI.

Sacrilegi sunt ecclesiarum predones unde in concilio Agathensi ... atque indubitanter infames sacrilegique habendi sunt.

(Burchard 11.28, PL 140.865, MC 45, p. 272, MC 44, p. 200)

⟨CLII⟩ De combustione ecclesie.

Iulii pape.

Si quis ecclesiam igne comburit quindecim annos ... restituat et pretium
p. 87 suum distribuat / pauperibus.

(Burchard 3.204, PL 140.713, MC 45, p. 146, MC 44, p. 119)

⟨CLIII⟩ Quod santum sanctorum sit quiquid deo offertur.

Ex decretis Bonifatii pape.

Nulli liceat ignorare omne quod domino ... iudicetur et si emendare noluerit excommunicetur.

(Burchard 11.17, PL 140.863, MC 45, p. 271, MC 44, p. 199)

⟨CLIV⟩ Synodus Hybernensis.

p. 88 Si quis ecclesiam dei per aliquam intentionem ... / ... et crebris ieiuniis et helemosinis atque orationibus peniteat.

(5L 4.113b, C. p. 229)

⟨CLV⟩ De distractione ecclesiasticarum rerum.

Ex concilio Bracarensi.

Quicumque presbiter de iure tituli sui ... et alienator honoris sui amissione mulcetur.

(Burchard 3.180, PL 140.708, MC 45, p. 142, MC 44, p. 117)

⟨CLVI⟩ Synodus Romana.

Si quis abbas rem mobilem sive immobilem ... acceptum tenuerit com-
p. 89 munione priva/tus sit fiat.

(cf. 5L 3.100, Forn. 362, C. p. 115)

⟨CLVII⟩ De sepulchro violatoribus.

Ex concilio Toletano.

Si quis clericus aut laicus in demoliendis ... ordine submoveri et penitentie triennio deputari.

(Burchard 11.63, PL 140. 871, MC 45, p. 276, MC 44, p. 203; 5L 4.133b, C. p. 235, attributed to Gregory; and cf. MC 554, p. 161, attributed to 'Concilio Toletano.')

⟨CLVIII⟩ De eo qui aream aut domum igne cremavit.

Gregorius.

Si quis aream aut domum cuiusque ... a humana diffinitionem iii. annos peniteat.

(5L 4.132b, C. p. 235)

⟨CLIX⟩ Ex decretis Iohannis pape.

Si quis monasteria et loca deo ... et velut sacrilegi canonice sententie subiugentur.

(Burchard 11.22, PL 140.864)

p. 90 ⟨CLX⟩ Ex penitentia Romana. /

Si aliquis de ministerio ecclesie quolibet modo aliquid furatus fuerit vii. annos peniteat.

(Burchard 11.65, PL 140.871, MC 45, p. 277, MC 44, p. 203; cf. 5L 4.124e, C. p. 233, attributed to Iudicium Theodori)

⟨CLXI⟩ De furto capitali.

Gregorius.

Si quis furtum capitale commiserit, id est aurum ... aliquid furtum faciens vii. dies peniteat.

(5L 4.125, C. p. 233, attributed to Gregory; and cf. Burchard 11.58, PL 140.870, attributed to Theodore, MC 45, p. 276, MC 44, p. 203)

⟨CLXII⟩ DE FURTO PER NECESSITATE FACTO.

Si quis per necessitatem furtatus fuerit cibaria ... hebdomadas tres si reddiderit, non cogatur ieiunare.

(Burchard 11.56, PL 140.869, MC 45, p. 275, MC 44, p. 202)

⟨CLXIII⟩ EX DICTIS GREGORII.

. 91 Quicumque furtivum comederit erit et sciat ... / ... de minoribus dictum est, si vero maior addantur.

(5L 4.127, C. p. 234)

⟨CLXIV⟩ SYNODUS ROMANA.

Si vult confiteri peccata sua sacerdoti ... ergo cor impenitens videtur illi esse.

(5L 4.129, C. p. 234)

⟨CLXV⟩ SYNODUS HIBERNENSI.

. 92 Si quis hominem gratis expoliaverit in via ... / ... censuram reconciliaverit fratri suo quem expoliavit.

(5L 4.135, C. p. 235)

⟨CLXVI⟩ EX CONCILIO AGATHENSI.

Si quis clericus aut monachus furtum ... levitate impleta penitentie satisfactione sola communio.

(Burchard 11.64, PL 140.871, MC 45, p. 276, MC 44, p. 203)

⟨CLXVII⟩ De sacrificio.

Iudicium Commeani.

p. 93 Si quis neglexerit sacrificium aut perdiderit ... / ... usque ad altare tantum lapsum fuerit superponat.

(5L 4.184b[1], C. p. 353)

⟨CLXVIII⟩ Ex decretis Pii pape.

p. 94 Si per negligentiam de calice aliquid ... / ... calicem subterposito et aquam ablutionis sumat.

(5L 4.184b[2], C. p. 353)

⟨CLXIX⟩ Gregorius.

p. 95 Si quis eucharistiam causa neglegentie perdiderit ... / ... et aqua ablutionis in ignem proiciatur.

(5L 4.184a, C. p. 352)

⟨CLXX⟩ Ex penitentiali Romano.

Si quis sacrificium vomuerit xl. dies ... noctem ii., si post matutinum una superpositio.

(5L 4.184c, C. p. 353, attributed to Iudicium canonum)

⟨CLXXI⟩ Ex decretis Euticiani pape.

p. 96 Qui acceperit sacrificium post cibum aut ... / ... maiores septem, clerici xx. dies peniteant.

(5L 4.361b [not in C]; cf. Burchard 5.35, PL 140.759; MC 45, p. 189, MC 44, p. 147)

⟨CLXXII⟩ EX CONCILIO CARAUSICO (*sic*).

Si quis sacerdos enormiter post solitum cibum ... vigiliis ex orationibus atque elemosinis peniteat.

(5L 4.186, C. p. 353, attributed to ⟨C ras⟩arausico)

⟨CLXXIII⟩ ITEM.

97 Si quis pro aqua vinum vino ... / ... intingere et sumere et unum annum peniteat.

(fons non invenitur)

⟨CLXXIV⟩ INTERROGATIO AUGUSTINI EPISCOPI ANGLORUM.

Si post illusionem que per sompnum ... si sacerdos sit sacra misteria celebrare.

(5L 5.100a, C. p. 317)

⟨CLXXV⟩ GREGORIUS.

99 Est in eadem illusionem necessaria valde ... / ... sacro misterio eo die abstinere oportet.

(cf. 5L 5.100a, C. p. 317)

⟨CLXXVI⟩ DE COTIDIANA PERCEPTIONE EUCHARISTIE.

EX DICTIS AUGUSTINI

100 Cotidie eucharistie communionem accipere nec laudo ... / ... in ora alia peccata non gravant.

(Burchard 5.15, PL 140.755; MC 45, p. 186, MC 44, p. 145)

⟨CLXXVII⟩ EX CONCILIO CESARAUGUSTANA

Qui euchastiam (*sic*) in ecclesiam accipiat et ... dictum est, placet et unum annum peniteat.

(5L 3.268.1,2, Forn. 446, C. p. 166)

⟨CLXXVIII⟩ UT QUI SEMPER PECCAT SI SEMPER ACCIPERE DEBENT.

Sanctus Cyprianus dixit: Eucharistia cotidie te cibum salutis accipitur.

(Burchard 5.18, PL 140.756, MC 45, p. 186, MC 44, p. 145)

p. 101 Sanctus Ambrosius dixit: Si quotiens/cumque effunditur sanguis Christi ... semper pecco, debeo semper habere medicinam.

(Burchard 5.18, PL 140.756, MC 45, p. 186, MC 44, p. 145)

Sanctus Hylarius episcopus dixit. Si non tanta sunt peccata ut ... iam peccare quievit communicare non desinat.

(Burchard 5.18, PL 140.756, MC 45, p. 186, MC 44, p. 145)

⟨CLXXIX⟩ EX DECRETIS SILVESTRI PAPE.

p. 102 Singulis dominicis diebus in quadragesima praeter illos ... / ... in natali domini penitus ab omnibus communicandum est.

(Burchard 5.19, PL 140.756, MC 45, p. 187 MC 44, p. 145)

⟨CLXXX⟩ EX DECRETIS SOTERIS PAPE.

In cena domini a quibusdam perceptio eucharistie ... ad percipienda corporis et sanguinis dominici sacramenta reconcilientur.

(Burchard 5.20, PL 140.756, MC 45, p. 187, MC 44, p. 145)

⟨CLXXXI⟩ EX CONCILIO CARTAGINENSIS.

Mulier enixa si vult communionem percipiat.

(Burchard 5.53, PL 140.762, MC 45, p. 192, MC 44, p. 149)

⟨CLXXXII⟩ DE EBRIETATE EX PENITENTIALI ROMANO.

Qui per ebrietatem vomitum facit, si presbiter ... si monachus xxx., si laicus xv.

(Burchard 14.13, PL 140.892, MC 45, p. 291, MC 44, p. 214)

103 ⟨CLXXXIII⟩ EX PENITENTIA BEDE. /

Laicus si per ebrietatem vomitum facit ... a carne et vino et cervisa abstineat.

(Burchard 14.14, PL 140.892, MC 45, p. 291, MC 44, p. 214)

⟨CLXXXIV⟩ EX EODEM

Si quis per nequitiam alium inebriat ... donec digne peniteat et emendationem promittat.

(Burchard 14.15, PL 140.892, MC 291, p. 18, MC 45, p. 215)

⟨CLXXXV⟩ EX DICTIS FRUCTUOSI EPISCOPI IN CANONE APOSTOLORUM.

Si quis ecclesiastica preditus ordinatione aut monachus ... in pane et aqua tribus mensibus peniteat.

(Burchard 14.9, PL 140.891, MC 45, p. 290, MC 44, p. 214)

Episcopus, presbiter, aut diaconus alee atque ebrietati ... aut communione privetur, similiter etiam laicus.

(Burchard 14.5, PL 140.891, MC 45, p. 290, MC 44, p. 213)

⟨CLXXXVI⟩ DE SORTILOGIS.

EX CONCILIO TOLETANO.

Si quis episcopus, presbiter, sive diaconus vel quilibet ex ordine clerico
104 rum ... / ...penitentie deditus scelus amissi sacrilegii luat.

(5L 3.336 Forn. 492, C. p. 183; and cf. Burchard 10.48, PL 140.851, MC 45, p. 162, MC 44, p. 193)

⟨CLXXXVII⟩ EX CONCILIO ANCIRITANO.

Qui auguria, auspicia sive somnia vel divinationes ... si vero seculares v. annos peniteant.

(5L 3.337, Forn. 493, C. p. 183)

⟨CLXXXVIII⟩ ITEM.

p. 105 Si quis mathematicus fuerit et per invocationem ... v. annos peniteat / ii. in pane et aqua.

(Paenitenitale Vallicellianum I, Schmitz 1.303)

⟨CLXXXIX⟩ EX CONCILIO TOLETANO.

Si aliquis manducat aut bibit aut portat ... magi et arioli et incantatores feriuntur.

(Burchard 10.25, PL 140.836, MC 45, p. 249, MC 44, p. 184)

⟨CXC⟩ EX PENITENTIALI ROMANO.

Mulier si divinationes vel incantationes diabolicas ... vel xl. dies secundum qualitatem delicti.

(Burchard 10.24, PL 140.836, MC 45, p. 248, MC 44, p. 184)

⟨CXCI⟩ EX PENITENTIALI THEODORI.

In tabulis vel codicibus sorte furtum ... divinationes aliquas in aliquibus rebus observet.

(Burchard 10.26, PL 140.836)

⟨CXCII⟩ DE ILLIS QUI AD FASCINUM INCANTAVERINT.

p. 106 Si quis precantaverint ad fascinum vel ... / ... cantatur tres quadragesimas in pane et aqua peniteat.

(Burchard 10.49, PL 140.851, MC 45, p. 262, MC 44, p. 193)

⟨CXCIII⟩ DE FALSIS PENITENTIBUS.

GREGORIUS.

p. 107 Falsas penitentias dicimus que non secundum auctoritatem ... / ... deus cor illius illustret ad penitentiam.

(MC 522, p. 185; Conc. Rom. c. 6, Gregory VII, Caspar, *Das Register Gregors VII*, book 6, p. 404)

⟨CXCIV⟩ DE ABSTINENTIA SABBATI.

Quia dies sabbati tempore sanctos patres nostros in abstinentia ... infirmitate impediente abstineat.

(MC 522, p. 186; Conc. Rom. c. 8, Gregory VII, Caspar, *Das Register Gregors VII*, book 6, p. 405)

⟨CXCV⟩ DE INFIRMIS IN PERICULO MORTIS CONSTITUTIS.

EX PENITENTIALI THEODORI.

p. 108 Ab infirmis in periculo mortis positis ... / ... secundum statuta sanctorum patrum communione viatici reficiantur.

(Burchard 18.14, PL 140.941, MC 45, p. 329, MC 44, p. 243)

⟨CXCVI⟩ EX DICTIS AUGUSTINI.

p. 109 Sane quisquis positus in ultima necessitate ... / ... peccata ad dimiserunt non tu peccata.

(Burchard 18.12, PL 140.940, MC 45, p. 329, MC 44, p. 243)

⟨CXCVII⟩ IDEM.

Si rem alienam propter quam peccatum ... si ut dixi cum restitui potest.

(Ivo, Dec. 15.25, PL 161.862)

⟨CXCVIII⟩ CELESTINUS PAPA.

Non debet episcopus aut presbiter aut diaconus commisceri ... si tamen in conscientia populi deverint.

(Polycarpus IV.41; Coll. Caesaraugustana [first version, MS. Salamanca Univ. Civil 2644, fol. 139v] XV.38 [and second version, MS Paris, BN lat. 3876, fol. 110v], XV.46; and Coll. Pragensis I [Praha, Národní Knihova Ceské Republiky, VIII.H.7, fol. 25r] 70; cf. Gratian C. XXX, q.1, c. 10)

⟨CXCIX⟩ IDEM.

p. 110 Si quis sacerdos cum filia spirituali fornicatus / ... ibique cunctis diebus vite sue serviat.

(5L 2.79, Forn. 227, C. p. 86)

⟨CC⟩ EX CONCILIO APUT VERMERIAM HABITO.

Si quis cum matre et filia fornicatus ... femine absque marito in perpetuum maneant.

(Burchard 17.12, PL 140.921, MC 45, p. 314, MC 44, p. 232)

⟨CCI⟩ EX EODEM.

p. 111 Si homo fornicatus fuerit cum muliere ... peniteat / et sine spe coniugii maneat.

(Burchard 17.13, PL 140.922, MC 45, p. 314, MC 44, p. 232)

⟨CCII⟩ DE RECONCILIATIONE PENITENTE AD MORTEM.

Leo episcopus Theodoro Foroiuliensi episcopo. His qui in tempore necessitatis et in periculi ... cum conversus ingemueris, tunc salvas eris.

(Burchard 18.4, PL 140.938, MC 45, p. 327, MC 44, p. 242)

p. 112 Ita ergo necessitatibus talium auxiliandum est ... / et penitentie et reconciliationis beneficium consequantur.

(Burchard 18.9, PL 140.940, MC 45, p. 328, MC 44, p. 242)

⟨CCIII⟩ QUOD NON SIT PORRIGENDA HOSTIA INTINCTA.

Illud quod per complemento communionis quidam intinctam ... non quod huius sacramenti institutionem signaret.

(Burchard 5.1, PL 140.751, MC 45, p. 183, MC 44, p. 143)

⟨CCIV⟩ URBANUS PAPA.

p. 114 Sanctorum patrum sententiis consona consentientes ex dei / ... ad subdiaconum unicam et virginem uxorem habuerit.

(Concilium. Melfi. [1089], cc. 1-3, ed. Somerville, 252 f., and see p. 187)

⟨CCV⟩ DE NUMERO MISSARUM.

ALEXANDER PAPA.

p. 115 Sufficit sacerdoti unam missam in die una ... / ... dicere preter si idem episcopus iusserit.

(Alexander II, Mansi 19.979; and Ivo, Dec. 2.81, PL 161.178)

⟨CCVI⟩ EX DICTIS ZACHARIE PAPE.

Episcopus aut presbiter dum ingressus fuerit missarum sollempnia cele-
p. 116 branda ... corpore et sanguine domini nostri Iesu Christi / sit suspensus.

(5L 3.235, Fom. 430, C. p. 161)

⟨CCVII⟩ EX CONCILIO SALEGUNSTAT.

Decretum est in eodem concilio ut presbiter aliquis post gallicantum ... non celebret, hiemantibus similiter nisi necessitas cogat.

(Conc. Seleg. (1023), c. 4, PL 140.1059, and see D. S. Taylor 'Der Micrologus Bernolds von Konstanz und der Codex Stuttgart, Württembergische Landesbibliothek HB VI 114,' *Deutsches Archiv* 52 [1996] 171-179)

⟨CCVIII⟩ DECRETUM GREGORIUS SEPTIMUS PAPA ET URBANUS SECUNDUS (*sic*).

Presbiterorum filios a sacri altaris ministeriis removendos ... canonicis regularibus religiose probati fuerint conversari.

(Conc. Melf. [1089], c. 14, ed. Somerville, 257, and see p. 187; Ivo, Dec. 6.410, PL 161.533)

⟨CCIX⟩ EX CONCILIO VALERITINO.

Qui oblationes defunctorum aut negant ecclesiis ... cum difficultate reddunt tamquam egentium neccatores excommunicentur.

(Burchard 3.142, PL 140.701, MC 45, p. 136, MC 44, p. 113)

⟨CCX⟩ EX DECRETIS FABIANI.

p. 117 Omnia que deo offeruntur consecrata habeantur ... / ... qui sponsus earum est auferuntur.

(Burchard 3.129, PL 140.698, MC 45, p. 132, MC 44, p. 111)

⟨CCXI⟩ IDEM.

Omnis decime terre sive de frugibus ... usque ad satisfactionem et emendationem congruam.

Burchard 3.130, PL 140.698, MC 45, p. 133, MC 44, p. 111)

p. 118 ⟨CCXII⟩ EX DICTIS / HORMISDE PAPE.

Quod non oporteat a septuagesima usque in octavis pasche ... celebrare quod si factum fuerit separentur.

(Burchard 9.4, PL 140.816, MC 45, p. 233, MC 44, p. 174)

⟨CCXIII⟩ EX CONCILIO CARTAGINENSEM.

Sponsus et sponsa cum benedicendi sunt ... nocte pro reverentia benedictionis in virginitate permaneant.

(Burchard 9.5, PL 140.816, MC 45, p. 233, MC 44, p. 174; cf. MC 541, p. 281)

⟨CCXIV⟩ EX DICTIS HORMISDE PAPA (*sic*).

Ut nullus fidelis cuiuscumque condicionis sit ... a sacerdote accepta publice nubat in domino.

(Burchard 9.3, PL 140.816, MC 45, p. 233, MC 44, p. 174)

⟨CCXV⟩ EX CONCILIO TOLETANO.

p. 119 Vidue si priusquam continentiam profiteantur nubere ... / ... parentum vel suam cogantur accipere maritos.

(Ivo, Dec. 8.18, PL 161.588)

⟨CCXVI⟩ EX CONCILIO PARISIACENSE.

Nullus aut viduam aut filiam extra parentum ... ab ecclesie communione remotus anathematis gladio feriatur.

(Ivo, Dec. 8.25, PL 161.589)

⟨CCXVII⟩ HYSIDORUS ETHIMOLOGIA.

Raptor publica penitentia multetur, raptam vero ... hoc se coniungere
p. 120 presumpserit utrique / anathemarizentur.

(Ivo, Dec. 8.26, PL 161.589)

⟨CCXVIII⟩ EX DICTIS IULII PAPE.

Et hoc quoque statutum est ut relictam ... quinta si inventi fuerint non separentur.

(Bonizo 9.24, [E. Perels, *Bonizo, Liber de Vita Christiana* (Texte zur Geschichte des römischen und kanonischen Rechts im Mittelalter, 1; Berlin, 1930), 286], Polycarpus VI 4, 5; Coll. 7 librorum [Torino, Biblioteca Nazionale Universitaria, D.IV.33, fol. 83r; cf. Gratian C. XXXV, q. 2-3, c. 12)

⟨CCXIX⟩ NOVELLARUM CONSTITUTIO.

Si quis divinis tactis scripturis iuraverit ... nulla dos, nulla scriptura alia interposita sit.

(cf. MC 215 Z, p. 185; Ivo, Dec. 16.142, PL 161.932, Pan. 6.7, PL 161.1245)

⟨CCXX⟩ AMBROSIUS.

Si tu abstines sine uxoris voluntate ... et peccatum illius tue imputabitur abstinentie.

(MC 215 Z, p. 194, attributed to Augustine; Ivo, Dec. 8.130, PL 161.612, Pan. 6.79, PL 161.1259)

⟨CCXXI⟩ INNOCENTII PAPE.

p. 121 De his etiam requisivit dilectio tua / ... nisi si incentores illiciti consortii fuisse denegantur.

(Burchard 9.72, PL 140.827, MC 45, p. 242, MC 44, p. 180)

⟨CCXXII⟩ EX CONCILIO CABILONENSI.

p. 122 Dictum etiam nobis est quasdam / feminas ... penitentiam agat, viro tamen suo non separetur.

(Burchard 17.23, PL 140.923, MC 45, p. 316, MC 44, p. 233)

⟨CCXXIII⟩ EX CONCILIO MOGATIENSI.

p. 123 De eo quod interrogastis si ille qui filiam suam duxit uxorem ... / ... penitentia multetur et sine spe coniugii maneat.

(Burchard 17.24, PL 140.924, MC 45, p. 316, MC 44, p. 233)

⟨CCXXIV⟩ EX CONCILIO TRIBULIENSI.

Nullus proprium filium aut filiam a fonte baptismatis ... episcopum tenuit, ubi autem factum fuerit separentur.

(Burchard 17.25, PL 140.924, MC 45, p. 316, MC 44, p. 233)

⟨CCXXV⟩ EX CONCILIO MELDENSI.

p. 124 Iis qui vivente marito coniugem illius ... / ... si alia ut diximus non impedierit ratio.

(Burchard 9.65, PL 140.826, MC 45, p. 240, MC 44, p. 180)

⟨CCXXVI⟩ EX CONCILIO TRIBURIENSI.

Relatum est auribus sanctorum sacerdotum quidam ulterius (*sic*) uxorem ... tale igitur conubium prohibemus et anathematizamus.

(Burchard 9.66, PL 140.826, MC 45, p. 241, MC 44, p. 180)

p. 125 ⟨CCXXVII⟩ EX CONCILIO APUD ALTEUM / ABITO PRESENTE CURRADO REGE.

Illud vero communi decreto secundum canonum instituta definimus et preiudicamus, ut si quis cum uxore alterius vivente eo ... coniugium quam prius polluit per adulterium.

(Burchard 9.74, PL 140.828, MC 45, p. 242, MC 44, p. 181)

⟨CCXXVIII⟩ NYCOLAUS PAPA.

Reverentissimo et sanctissimo Salomoni ecclesie Constantie episcopo illustri servus servorum dei sanctorum in celis societatem, siscitatur a no-
p. 126 bis sanctitas tua si aliquis ... / ...cum qua idem fuerat una caro effectus.

(MC 215 Z, p. 228, Ivo, Dec. 1.137, PL 161.92, 9.35, PL 161.664, Pan. 7.63, PL 161.1295)

⟨CCXXIX⟩ IDEM.

p. 127 Nosse desideras utrum mulier que viri ... / ... non habet sui corporis sed mulier.

(MC 215 Z, p. 212, Ivo, Dec. 1.136, PL 161.92, Pan. 6.124, PL 161.1276)

⟨CCXXX⟩ Ex concilio Arelatensi.

p. 128 Si unus ex coniugibus filium aut filiam ... / ...et mulier una caro effecti sunt.

(5L 5.118, C. p. 334)

⟨CCXXXI⟩ Ex dictis Augustini.

Per singulos menses gravia atque torpentia ... membrorum sanies corrupta degeneret.

(Ivo, Dec. 9.121, PL 161.688)

Anacletus servus Christi Iesu et ceteris cunctis fidelibus, qui abstulerit pa-
p. 129 tri vel matri aliquid ... / ... vel res ecclesie abstulerit sacrilegium facit.

(cf. Burchard 11.18, PL 140.863, MC 45, p. 271, MC 44, p. 199; Ivo, Dec. 14.88, PL 161.850)

p. 130 Si quis oblata deo dederit vel acceperit ... / ... accipienti vel danti vel possideati anathema.

(cf. Deusdedit 3.45, Glanville pp. 287 f.)

⟨CCXXXII⟩ De decima(i)s a laycis non accipiendis.

Decimas quas in usum pietatis concessas ... committere et eterne dampnationis periculum incurrere.

(MC 522, p. 185; and Firenze, Biblioteca Medicea Laurenziana, 16.15, fol. 100r; Gregory VII, Conc. Rom. [1078], c. 7; Caspar, *Das Register Gregors VII*, book VI, pp. 404 f.)

⟨CCXXXIII⟩ De clericis guadiam (*sic*) dent neque fideiussorem ponant.

Ut nullus presbiter vel diaconus seu subdiaconus vel de qualicumque cle-
p. 131 ricorum presumat legem / ... carrinas cum septem sequentibus annis peniteat.

(MC 522, p. 187; and Firenze, Biblioteca Medicea Laurenziana, 16.15 , fol. 100r, under a rubric 'Ut nullus clericus audeat legem facere et sacramentum iurare coram laica potestate absque presentia episcopi sui.' For these common canonical prohibitions, see *Capitula episcoporum I*, ed. P. Brommer [*Monumenta Germaniae Historica:* Hannover, 1984] 20, and citations therein.)

⟨CCXXXIV⟩ DE EODEM RE.

EX CONCILIO CARTAGINENSIS.

Clericus fideiussionibus inserviens abiciatur.

(Burchard 2.173, PL 140.654, MC 45, p. 93, MC 44, p. 83; 5L 1.230, Forn. 140, C. p. 58; and MC 541, p. 40)

⟨CCXXXV⟩ UT CIBIS SACERDOTUM SEMPER LECTIO DIVINA MISCEATUR.

EX CONCILIO AFRICANO.

Pro reverentia dei et sacerdotum id universa sancta synodus statuit, ut quia solent crebro mensis otiose ... sacerdotali convivio lectio sacrarum scripturarum misceatur.

(Burchard 2.169, PL 140.653, MC 45, p. 93, MC 44, p. 83)

⟨CCXXXVI⟩ DE CLERICIS IOCULARIBUS.

EX CONCILIO CARTAGINENSIS.

p. 132 / Clericos scurriles et verbis turpibus ioculatores ab officio detrahendos.

(Burchard 2.172, PL 140.654, MC 45, p. 93, MC 44, p. 83; 5L 3.246.1 Forn. 435, C. p. 162; and MC 554, p. 162; and MC 541, pp. 215, 262; and cf. MC 297, p. 230)

⟨CCXXXVII⟩ DE SECULARIBUS ECCLESIAM VEL CLERICUM INIUSTE CALUMPNIANTIBUS.

Si quis secularium pro calumpma ecclesiam ... catholicorum comunione nisi digne penituerit arceatur.

(Burchard 15.5, PL 140.895, MC 45, p. 293, MC 44, p. 216)

⟨CCXXXVIII⟩ UT NULLUS SECULARIS ALICUI EX CLERICO VIM INFERRE PRESUMANT.

EX CONCILIO APUD THEODOTISVILLA.

Quicumque iudex aut secularis presbitero ... iniurium ferre presumpserit anathema habeatur.

(Burchard 16.36, PL 140.918, MC 45, p. 311, MC 44, p. 229)

⟨CCXXXIX⟩ DE ILLIS QUI PRESBITEROS SUOS MALE TRACTAVERINT.

p. 133 Si quis presbiterum inhonorat aut verbo ... / ... qui presunt duplici honore digni habeantur.

(Burchard 2.229, PL 140.664, MC 45, p. 113, MC 44, p. 92)

⟨CCXL⟩ UT NULLUS IN DOMINICIS DIEBUS GENUA FLECTAT.

EX CONCILIO NICENO.

Quoniam sunt quidam qui die dominico ... debeant deo tantummodo vota persolvere.

(5L 3.62, Forn. 342, C. p. 132)

⟨CCXLI⟩ DE LETANIA MAIORE QUOMODO OBSERVANDA SIT.

EX CONCILIO MOGATIENSI.

Placuit nobis ut letania maior observanda sit a cunctis ... et cilicio induti nisi infirmitas impedierit.

(Burchard 13.6, PL 140.886, MC 45, p. 286, MC 44, p. 211)

p. 134 ⟨CCXLII⟩ DE IEIUNIO / ROGATIONUM.

EX CONCILIO AURELIANO.

Agamus hos dies cum summa reverentia ... dies enim sunt abstinentie non letitie.

(Burchard 13.7, PL 140.886, MC 45, p. 287, MC 44, p. 211)

⟨CCXLIII⟩ DE CLERICIS QUI AD SACRIFICIUM COTIDIE VENIRE NEGLEGUNT.

EX CONCILIO TOLETANO.

Presbiter vel diaconus vel subdiaconus vel quilibet ecclesie deputatus clericus ... clericus non habeatur, *sic* castigatus non emendaverit.

(Burchard 2.152, PL 140.650, MC 45, p. 90, MC 44, p. 81; and cf. 5L 3.184, Forn. 399, C. p. 150)

Clericus qui intra muros civitatis manet et ea die ... septem dies a communione habeatur extraneus.

(Burchard 2.153, PL 140.651, MC 45, p. 90, MC 44, p. 81)

⟨CCXLIV⟩ QUOD INTER CATHOLICA HABEATUR QUI IN PASCHA, PENTECOSTE, ET NATALIS DOMINI NON COMMUNICAT.

p. 135 EX CONCILIO AGATHENSIS. /

Seculares vero qui in natalis domini ... non credantur nec inter catholicos habeantur.

(Burchard 5.23, PL 140.757, MC 45, p. 187, MC 44, p. 146; and cf. 5L 3.267, Forn. 446, C. p. 166)

⟨CCXLV⟩ DE CLERICIS INTEMPERATE INVENTE.

EX CONCILIO CARTAGINENSIS.

Clerici inter epulas cantantes ab officio detrahendi sunt.

(Burchard 2.170, PL 140.654, MC 45, p. 93, MC 44, p. 83; MC 554, p. 56, MC 541, pp. 219, 262, and MC 372, p. 109; and cf. 5L 3.246.2 Forn. 435, C. p. 163)

⟨CCXLVI⟩ DE EODEM.

Si quis clericus aut monachus verba scurrilia risumque moventia loquitur acerrime corripiatur.

(Burchard 2.171, PL 140.654, MC 45, p. 93, MC 44, p. 83)

⟨CCXLVII⟩ ITEM DE EODEM.

Clericus nec comam nutriat nec barbam.

(Burchard 2.174, PL 140.654, MC 45, p. 93, MC 44, p. 84)

⟨CCXLVIII⟩ DE CLERICIS ADULATORIBUS ET PRODITORIBUS.

Synodus Cartaginiensi. Clericus qui adulationibus et proditionibus vacare deprehenditur degradetur ab officio.

(Burchard 2.176, PL 140.654, MC 45, p. 93, MC 44, p. 84; 5L 4.223g, C. p. 263, MC 541, p. 262)

⟨CCXLIX⟩ DE ORDINATIS SI USURAS EXCREVERINT.

EX CANONE APOSTOLORUM.

Episcopus, presbiter aut diaconus usuras a debitoribus exigens aut desinat aut certe dampnetur.

(Burchard 2.119, PL 140.646, MC 45, p. 86, MC 44, p. 78; and 5L 4.174c, C. p. 349)

⟨CCL⟩ EX CONCILIO AURELIANO.

p. 136 Ut presbiteri a turpibus lucris et usuris ... etiam plebes sibi / subditas abstinere instruant.

(Burchard 2.125, PL 140.647, MC 45, p. 87, MC 44, p. 79)

⟨CCLI⟩ EX CONCILIO CARTAGINENSI.

Ut clericus si commendaverit pecuniam, pecuniam accipiat, si speciem, eamdem speciem quantum dederit accipere.

(Burchard 2.124, PL 140.647, MC 45, p. 87, MC 44, p. 79)

⟨CCLII⟩ De illis qui invident fratrum provectionibus.

Ex concilio Africano.

Clericus invidens fratrum provectionibus donec in vitio est non promoveatur.

(Burchard 2.16, PL 140.628, MC 45, p. 69, MC 44, p. 65)

⟨CCLIII⟩ Ut seditionarii non ordinentur.

Ex eodem.

Seditionarios nunquam ordinandos clericos sicut nec usurarios vel iniuriarum suarum ultores.

(Burchard 2.17, PL 140.628, MC 45, p. 69, MC 44, p. 66)

⟨CCLIV⟩ De violatore ecclesie.

Synodus Romana.

Si quis ecclesie dei nequiter violator ... templum dei violaverit disperdet illum deus.

(5L 4.113, C. p. 229)

⟨CCLV⟩ Ex concilio Triburiensi.

Si quis in atrio ecclesie pugnam committit ... altario solvatur cuiuscum-
p. 137 que fuerit / ecclesia illa.

(Burchard 3.196, PL 140.711, MC 45, p. 145, MC 44, p. 118)

⟨CCLVI⟩ De eadem re.

Iudicium sinodali.

Ecclesia que ab adulteriis contaminata fuerit ... aspergatur et fiat ut antea sacrificata.

(fons non invenitur)

⟨CCLVII⟩ De fugientibus ad ecclesiam.

Ex concilio Arausico.

Eos qui ad ecclesiam confugerit tradi ... per omnes ecclesias disstrictissima dampnationem feriatur.

(Burchard 3.195, PL 140.711, MC 45, p. 145, MC 44, p. 118)

⟨CCLVIII⟩ De eodem.

Ex concilio apud Theodotisvillam.

p. 138 Reum confugientem ad ecclesiam sue in atrium ... / ... magistris ecclesie obedire noluerit canonice constringatur.

(Burchard 3.194, PL 140.711, MC 45, p. 144, MC 44, p. 118)

⟨CCLIX⟩ De his qui per sue tiranidis patentiam contra domini atque sancte ecclesie cuiuslibet gradu mittere manum ausus fuerit.

Ex concilio Laodicensi.

p. 140 Quod si quis dei sancteque ecclesie extiterit ... / ... traditor dampnationis sustinent penam cum suis omnibus.

(5L 4.114b, C. p. 229)

p. 141 E contra qui non dei sancteque ecclesie contemptor ... / ... de quibusdam, gravibus de quibusdam levibus causis.

(5L 4.114b, C. p. 229)

⟨CCLX⟩ Si quis inter celebranda divina misteria ministris dei iniuriam fecerit.

Iustinianus imperator.

p. 142 Si quis dum divina misteria celebrantur ... / ... solum civiles sed etiam militares iudices.

(5L 3.183, Forn. 399, C. p. 149)

⟨CCLXI⟩ DE INFANTIS EX ADULTERIO NATIS ET AD ECCLESIAM EXPOSITIS.

EX CONCILIO ARELATENSIS.

Si expositis ante ecclesiam cuiusque fuerit miseratione ... districtione dampnabitur sicut patrum sancxit auctoritas.

(Burchard 3.201, PL 140.712, MC 45, p. 145, MC 44, p. 119)

⟨CCLXII⟩ DE RAPTORE SI CUM RAPTA AD ECCLESIAM CONFUGERIT.

EX CONCILIO AURELIANO.

De raptoribus autem feminarum id constituendum esse censuimus, ut si
p. 143 ad ecclesiam ... / ... mulieris ecclesiasticis viris obedire noluerint excommunicentur.

(Burchard 3.191, PL 140.710, MC 45, p. 144, MC 44, p. 118; cf. 5L 5.20d, C. p. 274)

⟨CCLXIII⟩ UT NULLUS ALIQUID MUNUS PROPTER ECCLESIA A PRESBITERO REQUIRAT.

EX CONCILIO ROTOMAGENSIS.

Sancitum est atque omnibus modis prohibitum, ut si quis presbiter inventum fuerit ... a clero et alienus existat a regula.

(Burchard 3.114, PL 140.695, MC 45, p. 130, MC 44, p. 109)

⟨CCLXIV⟩ UT NULLUS PRESBITER TITULUM USURPARE PRESUMAT.

p. 144 Ut si quilibet presbiterorum defunctus fuerit ... / ... illam nequaquam optineat quam usurpare teptavit (*sic*).

(Burchard 3.229, PL. 140.722, MC 45, p. 155, MC 44, p. 125)

⟨CCLXV⟩ QUID EPISCOPO AGENDUM SIT SI PLURES HEREDES DE UNA CONTENDERINT ECCLESIA.

EX CONCILIO TRIBURENSI

Si plures heredes contenderint de communi ecclesia ... statuant ibi presbiterum et unde vivat.

(Burchard 3.40, PL 140.679, MC 45, p. 115, MC 44, p. 100)

⟨CCLXVI⟩ DE OBSERVANDA MENSA CHRISTI.

EX CONCILIO GANGRENSI.

p. 145 Observandum est, ut mensa Christi, id est altare ubi corpus ... / ... in mundo loco sub serratura recondatur.

(Burchard 3.97, PL 140.693, MC 45, p. 127, MC 44, p. 108)

⟨CCLXVII⟩ UT CORPORALE EX PURISSIMO LINTEO SIT ET UNIUS MATERIE.

EX CONCILIO GANGRENSI.

p. 146 Corporale super quod sacra oblatio immolatur ... / ... post hec a lavandario in nitido loco paretur.

(Burchard 3.98, PL 140.693, MC 45, p. 128, MC 44, p. 108)

⟨CCLXVIII⟩ UT LAICI IUXTA ALTARE NON SEDEANT.

EX CONCILIO MOGATIENSI.

Ut laici secus altare quo sacra misteria ... feminis sicut mos pateant sancta sanctorum.

(Burchard 3.102, PL 140.693, MC 45, p. 128, MC 44, p. 108)

⟨CCLXIX⟩ DE CLERICIS FUGITIVIS NE AB ALIIS RECIPIATUR (*sic*).

EX CONCILIO AURELIANENSI.

In concilio Antioceno simul et in Calcedonensi precipitur, ut fugitivi cleri-
p. 147 ci et peregrini ... / ... et sui episcopi vel abbatis licentiam.

(Burchard 2.138, PL 140.648, MC 45, p. 88, MC 44, p. 80)

⟨CCLXX⟩ DE EADEM RE.

EX CONCILIO CARTAGINENSI.

Clericis sine commendaticiis litteris episcopi sui ... monachiis quoque presentis sententiae forma servetur.

(Burchard 2.142, PL 140.649, MC 45, p. 88, MC 44, p. 80)

⟨CCLXXI⟩ UT CLERICI NEC VIRI RELIGIOSI ANTE HORAM TERTIAM INHIANTUR CONVIVIT.

EX CONCILIO CARTAGINENSI.

Non oportet clericos vel laicos religiosos ante sacram horam ... post cibos gratias autori (*sic*) deo referre.

(Burchard 2.165, PL 140.653, MC 45, p. 92, MC 44, p. 83; 5L 4.193f., C. p. 359)

⟨CCLXXII⟩ DE HIS QUI ECCLESIASTICA IEIUNIA ABSQUE NECESSITATE DISSOLUUNT.

EX CONCILIO GANGRENSI.

Si quis eorum qui continentie student ... stimulo cogitationis sue impul-
p. 148 sus / anathema sit.

(5L 4.193g, C. p. 359; Burchard 13.5, PL 140.885, MC 45, p. 286, MC 44, p. 211)

⟨CCLXXIII⟩ QUOD NON OPORTEAT IN BIGAMI NUPTIIS ORARE PRESBITERUM.

EX CONCILIO NEOCERENSI.

Presbiterum in nuptiis bigami prandere non convenit ... convivium talibus nuptiis possit prebere consensum.

(Burchard 2.133, PL 140.648, MC 45, p. 88, MC 44, p. 79; cf. 5L 5.21, C. p. 276)

⟨CCLXXIV⟩ DE HIS QUI VELUT PECCATUM COPULAM DESERUNT NUPTIARUM.

EX CONCILIO GANGRENSI.

Si qua mulier virum proprium relinquens discedere voluerit nuptias execrata anathema sit.

(Ivo Dec. 8.229, PL 161.633; and cf. MC 541, p. 274, Coll. Dionysio-Hadriana)

⟨CCLXXV⟩ De ordine quo de depositi iniuste iterum ordinentur.

Ex concilio Toletano et in sancta synodo.

p. 149 Episcopus, presbiter, aut diaconus si a gradu suo iniuste ... / ... reparatione sui recipiant quod cum ordinarentur perceperant.

(5L 2.89, Forn. 233, C. p. 91; and Burchard 2.192, PL 140.657, MC 45, p. 96, MC 44, p. 86)

⟨CCLXXVI⟩ De his qui sine baptismate moriuntur.

Iudicium Theodori.

Cuius parvulus per neglegentiam sine baptisimo ... donis gratie eum fraudavit unde eterna requie exclusus est.

(5L 3.46.1,2; Forn. 334, C. p. 128)

⟨CCLXXVII⟩ Ut post baptisma crisma detur.

Concilio Laodocense.

p. 150 Quod oporteat eos qui baptizantur / post lavacrum chrisma celeste percipere et regni Christi participes inveniri.

(5L 3.20, Forn. 324, C. p. 127; and Burchard 4.65, PL 140.739; MC 45, p. 172 MC 44, p. 146)

⟨CCLXXVIII⟩ De baptizato et non chrismato ab episcopo si moritur.

Concilio Arausico.

De eo qui in baptismate quacumque necessitate faciente non chrismatis fuerit, in confirmatione sacerdotis commovebitur.

(5L 3.27, 3.47, Forn. 326, 334, C. pp. 127, 128)

⟨CCLXXIX⟩ DE EADEM RE.

Si cuius parvulus per neglegentiam sine chrismate ... iii. annos peniteat, si vero sine neglegentia.

(5L 3.47.1, Forn. 334, C. p. 128)

⟨CCLXXX⟩ DE OPERIBUS DIEI DOMINICI.

IUDICIUM CANONUM.

Qui operatur die dominico septem dies peniteat, lavacrum capitis et pedis die dominico licet.

(5L 3.57, Forn. 340, C. p. 131)

⟨CCLXXXI⟩ DE REBUS PER TRIGINTA ANNOS POSSESSIS

Et de rebus ecclesiarum que ab eis ... ad fiscum dominicum pertinentes
p. 151 contineri solent. /

(Burchard 3.150, PL 140.702, MC 45, p. 136, MC 44, p. 113)

⟨CCLXXXII⟩ CONCILIO CALCEDONENSI.

Singularum ecclesiarum rusticas parrochias vel possessiones ... provincie de his movere certamen decrevimus.

(Burchard 3.148, PL 140.702, MC 45, p. 136, MC 44, p. 113)

⟨CCLXXXIII⟩ DE NAUFRAGIO POST EVASIONEM MARIS.

HENRICI IMPERATORIS PRIMI.

Si quis naufragios post maris evasionem ... aliquid malo ordine tractare anathema sit.

(5L 3.211, Forn. 412, C. p. 155)

⟨CCLXXXIV⟩ DE CLERICIS DIMISSIS.

p. 152 Synodus Romana. Si quis a se vel a parentibus ... / ... et octo patrum anathemate maledictionis maneat.

(5L 3.210, Forn. 412, C. p. 155)

⟨CCLXXXV⟩ DE ABBATE VEL MONACHUS QUI PRESUMUNT FILOS DE BAPTISMO SUSCIPERE.

CONCILIO URBICO.

Non liceat abbas filios de baptismo suscipere ... mensibus in alio monasterio retrudatur.

(5L 2.194, Forn. 291, C. p. 117)

p. 153 ⟨CCLXXXVI⟩ DE PERDITO COMMENDA/TO REDDENDO.

Synodus Sardicensis. Si quis commendavit pecuniam placuit ut accipiat qui commendavit.

(5L 4.119b, C. p. 231)

⟨CCLXXXVII⟩ DE COMMENDATIS PER FURTUM RAPTIS AB ECCLESIA CATHOLICA NON REDDENDIS.

SYNODUS HYBERNENSIS.

Omne depositum redditur nisi depositum ecclesie ... sint perdita sed de se non debet.

(5L 4.120, C. p. 232)

⟨CCLXXXVIII⟩ DE EADEM RE.

Si quis custodierit clavem domus et fur ... quanto magis si cum pecunia
p. 154 sua furatum sit. /

(5L 4.120, C. p. 232)

⟨CCLXXXIX⟩ CONSTITUTA GREGORII PAPE.

p. 155 i. Si quis presbiteram duxerit in coniugium ... / ... xiiii. Si quis ex clericis relaxaverit comam, anathema sit.

(74T, cc. 276-289; and cf. MC 554, p. 46, MC 1, p. 401, 402, and MC 439, p. 220)

⟨CCXC⟩ DE HIS QUI AD MERCEDEM IEIUNAVERINT.

Synodus Romana. Si quis ad mercedem ieiunaverit si per ignorantiam
p. 156 ... / autem per industriam hoc presumitur anathematizetur.

(5L 4.47, C. p. 209)

⟨CCXCI⟩ DE DISCRETIONE PENITENTIE.

GREGORIUS.

p. 158 Ponunt canones peccantibus de quibusdam peccatis ... / ... traxit ad culpam afflictam reducat adveniam.

(5L 4.21, C. p. 199)

⟨CCXCII⟩ DE REDEMPTIONE PENITENTIE.

Pro uno die quem in pane et aqua ... sive tres tamen velut facultas hominum est.

(5L 4.46, C. p. 208)

p. 161 Si quis ieiunare non potest pro uno anno ... / est non remittetur ei neque hic neque in futuro.

(5L 4.46, C. p. 208)

⟨CCXCIII⟩ DE ILLIS QUI IEIUNARE NON POSSUNT ET NON HABENT UNDE REDIMERE POSSINT.

Qui ieiunare non potest et non habet ... et per singulo(a)s genuflexiones, Pater noster decantet.

(Burchard 19.24, PL 140.983, MC 45, p. 358, MC 44, p. 266)

⟨CCXCIV⟩ ALIO MODO.

Qui autem psalmos nescit per uno die ... et per singulas genuflexiones, Pater noster decantet.

(cf. Burchard 19.15, PL 140.982, MC 45, p. 357, MC 44, p. 265; and Theodore Cant. Capit, c. 10, PL 99.940)

⟨CCXCV⟩ ALIO MODO.

p. 162 Duodecim triduane singule cum psalteriis tribus ... per singula / psalteria, excusant unius anni penitentie.

(cf. Theodore Cant., c. 10, PL 99.940; and. Paenitentiale Bedae, Schmitz 1.563)

⟨CCXCVI⟩ ITEM.

Ut viginti quattuor biduane similiter cum tribus ... per singula psalteria excusant duos annos.

(cf. Theodore Cant., c. 10, PL 99.940; and. Paenitentiale Bedae, Schmitz 1.563)

⟨CCXCVII⟩ ALIO MODO.

Septuaginta quinque psalmi cum cotidem veniis ... et cum palmatas trecentis excusant triduanas.

(cf. Theodore Cant., c. 10, PL 99.940; and Paenitentiale Bedae, Schmitz 1.563)

⟨CCXCVIII⟩ ITEM ALIO MODO.

Centum soleri dati in elemosinam unum annum ... xx. palmatas valere pro uno die.

(cf. Theodore Cant., c. 10, PL 99.940)

⟨CCXCIX⟩ DE PENITENTIA. ILLIUS ANNI QUI IN PANE ET AQUA IEIUNANDUS EST, ISTO ORDINE OBSERVARI DEBET.

EX PENITENTIALI ROMANO.

p. 164 Penitentia unius anni qui in pane et aqua ... / ... et ventris distentionem semper in omnibus caveat.

(Burchard 19.9, PL 140.980, MC 45, p. 356, MC 44, p. 264)

Iste annus secundus est ab illo anno ... committunt et qui alia huiusmodi perpetraverunt.

(Burchard 19.10, PL 140.981, MC 45, p. 356, MC 44, p. 264)

p. 165 Penitentia illius anni talis esse debet ... / ... sicut in superiori capitulo notatum est peragat.

(cf. Burchard 19.10, PL 140.981, MC 45, p. 356, MC 44, p. 264)

Solus Romanus pontifex universalis habetur teste Calcedonensi concilio.

p. 169 ... / ... HE SUNT PROPRIE AUCTORITATES A APOSTOLICE SEDIS.

(Proprie auctoritates apostolice sedis, ed. H. Mordek, 'Proprie auctoritates apostolice sedis. Ein zweiter Dictatus papae Gregors VII?' *Deutsches Archiv* 28 [1972] 126-132; and see M. Wojtowytsch, 'Proprie auctoritates apostolice sedis: Bemerkungen zu einer bisher unbeachteten Überlieferung,' *Deutsches Archiv* 40 [1984] 616-619)

⟨CCC⟩

Loca humandi corporis pretio non possunt adipisci.

(5L 3.312, Forn. 469, C. p. 173)

⟨CCCI⟩ DE PRIMATU ROMANE ECCLESIE.

p. 170 Anacletus servus servorum dei / omnibus episcopis et reliquis Christi sacerdotibus salutem. Sacrosancta Romana et apostolica ecclesia non ab apostolis ... ad capud referte ut apostolico terminentur iudicio.

(74T, c. 2, Gilchrist 20)

⟨CCCII⟩ ITEM DE EODEM.

Silvester papa in generali residens synodo dixit: Nemo iudicavit primam
p. 171 sedem iustitiam temperari ... / a regibus neque a populo iudex iudicabitur.

(74T, c. 8, Gilchrist 23)

⟨CCCIII⟩ DE EODEM.

Iulius apostolice sedis episcopus omnibus episcopis. Habet sacrosancta Romana ecclesia potestatem singulari ... claudere ianuas celestis regni quibus voluerit.

(74T, c. 9, Gilchrist 23)

⟨CCCIV⟩ ITEM DE EODEM.

Symmachus papa universis episcopis. Aliorum hominum causas deus voluit ... discussoris indagini inviolatam exhibere conscientiam.

(74T, c. 11, Gilchrist 24)

⟨CCCV⟩ DE PRIVILEGIORUM AUCTORITATE.

Anacletus servus servorum dei omnibus episcopis et reliquis Christi
p. 172 sacerdotibus salutem. Privilegia ecclesiarum / et monasteriorum intemerata et ... firmamus auctoritate et peregrina iudicia submovemus.

(74T, c. 24, Gilchrist 33)

⟨CCCVI⟩ ITEM DE EODEM.

Gregorius Romane ecclesie presul Johanni Scintillano episcopo. Grave nimis et contra sacerdotale constat ... sunt pro quiete disposita niti deducere.

(74T, c. 27, Gilchrist 34)

Leo papa Marciano augusto. Privilegia ecclesiarum et monasteriorum

p. 173 sanctorum patrum ... / ... sanctionum nobis consentientibus vel neglegentibus violentur.

(74T, c. 25, Gilchrist 33)

⟨CCCVII⟩ De eodem re.

Gregorius papa omnibus episcopis. Rationis ordo non patitur ut monasterium ... disponendum arbitrium suum quisquam debeat vindicare.

(74 T, c. 31, Gilchrist 36)

⟨CCCVIII⟩ De monachorum monasteriorumque libertate.

Gregorius episcopus episcopis omnibus. Quam sit necessarium monaste-
p. 179 riorum quieti prospicere ... / ... numero quattuor die nonas aprili (*sic*) indictione quarta.

(74T, c. 39, Gilchrist 39)

⟨CCCIX⟩ De eodem.

Leo episcopus servus servorum dei omnibus Christi fidelibus salutem cum benedictione apostolica. Quotiens cumque a sede apostolica aliqua
p. 181 ... / ... dampnationis reus Iude proditori comparandum decernimus.

(74T, Rome, Biblioteca Casanatense, 2010, Gilchrist xlv)

⟨CCCX⟩ Quod liceat monachis cum sacerdotali officio ubique mini
p. 182 strare. /

Bonifatius papa episcopis omnibus. Sunt nonnullo fulti dogmate audacis-
p. 183 sime ... / ... quia quanto quisque excelsior tanto plus potentior.

(Ps.-Boniface IV (JE +1996), on which see J. Gilchrist, 'The Influence of the Monastic Forgeries attributed to Pope Gregory I [JE +1951] and Boniface IV [JE +1996],' in *Fälschungen im Mittelalter, Internationaler Kongress der Monumenta Germaniae historica, 16.-19. September 1986; Teil II. Gefälschte Rechtstexte, Der bestrafte Fälscher, Monumenta Germaniae Historica, Schriften* Band 33, II [Hannover, 1988] 272)

⟨CCCXI⟩ De libertate casinensis cenobii a⟨c⟩cellarum(?) eius.

Iohannes episcopus servus servorum dei Ragemprando religioso abbati
Casinensis. Per huius nostri apostolici privilegii sancimus ut loca que pre-
p. 184 phato beati Benedicti monasterio concessa sunt ... / ... infringere temp-
taverit anathema sit nisi resipuerit.

(Italia Pontificia 8, p. 127)

⟨CCCXII⟩ Item de eodem.

Sergius presul servus servorum dei Leoni abbati venerabili monasterii
sancti Benedicti Casinensis. Quemadmodum antecessores nostri eorum
p. 185 privilegiis antecessoribus ... / ... et reliquas introducere sanctorum et
baptismum facere.

(Italia Pontificia 8, p. 127)

⟨CCCXIII⟩ De eodem.

Gregorius papa omnibus episcopis. Si quis Normannorum vel quorumlibet hominum predia monasteria beati Benedicti montis Casinensis invaserit ... subiacet donec resipiscat et ecclesie satisfaciat.

(MC 522, p. 182, Conc. Rom. c. 2, Caspar, *Das Register Gregors VII*, book VI, p. 403; and Italia Pontificia 8, p. 147)

⟨CCCXIV⟩ Item.

Leo episcopus servus servorum dei karissimo filio Richerio venerabili et
religioso abbati. Postulastis a nobis quatinus concederemus et confirma-
p. 188 remus ... / ... se nisi resipuerit anathematis vinculis inodatum.

(cf. Italia Pontificia 8, p. 137, and PL 143.604)

⟨CCCXV⟩ De ordine accusationis deque accusatorum personis.

Anacletus urbis Rome episcopus omnibus episcopis. Accusandi vel testificandi licentia denegetur his ... normam aut regulariter prohibita neglexerint.

(74T, c. 44, Gilchrist 44)

⟨CCCXVI⟩ ITEM DE EODEM.

p. 189 Accusatores et testes esse non possunt ... / ... affectus querendus est et non suspectus.

(74T, c. 45, Gilchrist 45; and cf. Burchard 1.152, PL 140.594, MC 45, p. 40, MC 44, p. 44)

⟨CCCXVII⟩ DE EODEM RE.

Thelesphorus Rome archiepiscopus universis episcopis. Sicut laici et seculares homines volunt ... clerici debent eos recipere infamationibus suis.

(74T, c. 46, Gilchrist 45)

⟨CCCXVIII⟩ ITEM.

Stephanus Romane ecclesie episcopus dilectissimo fratri atque familiari
p. 191 amico Ylario. Infames esse personas dicimus que per aliqua culpa ... / ...
ad testimonium ullatenus possunt iuxte recipi.

(74T, c. 51, Gilchrist 47; and cf. Burchard 1.173, PL 140.599, MC 45, p. 46, MC 44, p. 48)

⟨CCCXIX⟩ ITEM DE EODEM.

Calixtus papa dilectis episcopis per Gallias constitutis. Rimande sunt accusatorum enucleatim persone qui ... consanguinei adversus extraneos testimonium non dicant.

(74T, c. 48, Gilchrist 46)

⟨CCCXX⟩ ITEM.

p. 192 Silvester papa in generali residens synodo / dixit: Nemo clericus vel diaconus vel presbiter propter quamlibet causam ... clericus accusans clericum curia introierit anathema sit.

(74T, c. 61, Gilchrist 52)

⟨CCCXXI⟩ UT INFRA PROVINCIAM ACCUSATIO TERMINETUR ET QUID SIT PROVINCIAM.

Cornelius episcopus Rufo coepiscopo. Nullus sacerdotum causam suam
p. 193 alieno committat ... / ... hec precepta non observaverit hostis est anime sue.

(74T, c. 62, Gilchrist 52)

⟨CCCXXII⟩ DE HISQUE SERVUS DEI PERSEQUUNTUR VEL DE HONESTANTUR.

Alexander episcopus omnibus orthodoxis. Pervenit ad conscientiam apo-
p. 194 stolice sedis quod / nonnulli ... a li/minibus ecclesie ad satisfactionem
p. 195 fieri.

(cf. MC 1, p. 43; Hinschius, pp. 95-97; Coll. Anselmo dedicata II.122; Bonizo 3.39, Perels, p. 84)

⟨CCCXXIII⟩ DE EODEM.

Procul dubio hii qui eos persequuntur ... infamia et exilio digni iudicantur finitimo.

(MC 1, p. 43; Hinschius, p. 96)

⟨CCCXXIV⟩ DE ILLIS SACERDOTIBUS QUI MORIENTIBUS PENITENTIAM DENEGAVERINT.

Iulius apostolice sedis episcopus omnibus episcopis. Si quis presbiter penitentiam abnegaverit morientibus ... in paradyso in hora ultima confessione.

(Burchard 18.21, PL 140.942, MC 45, p. 330, MC 44, p. 244)

⟨CCCXXV⟩ QUOD NULLI ULTIMA PENITENTIA SIT DENEGANDA.

Celestinus papa omnibus sacerdotibus Christi. Agnovimus penitentiam
p. 196 morientibus denegari / nec illorum ... / ...morienti sufficere vel momen-
p. 197 to posse non credidit.

(Burchard 18.22, PL 140.942, MC 45, p. 331, MC 44, p. 244; 5L 4.31, C. p. 203; and MC 1, p. 217 and MC 541, pp. 99, 162)

⟨CCCXXVI⟩ DE OBSERVATIONE QUATTUOR TEMPORUM.

Urbanus papa omnibus Christianis. Statuimus ut ieiunia quattuor temporum hoc ordine ... septembris et decembris more solito fiant.

(Concilium Placentinum [1095] c. 14, Weiland, Constit. 563, and see Somerville, p. 187)

⟨CCCXXVII⟩ UT RES NAUFRAGORUM NEMO RAPIT.

Paschalis papa omnibus orthodoxis. Quicumque res naufragorum diripiunt ut raptores et fratrum necatores ab ecclesie liminibus excludantur.

(Concilium Lateranense [1110] c. 7, Paschal II, ed. Blumenthal, 120; and see Somerville, p. 187)

⟨CCCXXVIII⟩ UT SI ALTARE MOTUM FUERIT DENUO ECCLESIA CONSECRETUR.

Ygynus papa episcopis omnibus. Si motum fuerit altare denuo consecre
p. 198 tur ecclesia ... / ... fuerit diligentissime expurgetur et denuo consecretur.

(Burchard 3.11, 12, PL 140.675, MC 45, p. 112, MC 44, p. 98; and cf. 5L 1.180, Forn. 116, C. p. 49, attributed to Pope Vigilius)

⟨CCCXXIX⟩ UT SINE MISSA ECCLESIA NON CONSECRARETUR.

Evaristus papa omnibus episcopis. Omnes basilice cum missa debent semper consecrari.

(Burchard 3.27 PL 140.677, MC 45, p. 113, MC 44, p. 99)

⟨CCCXXX⟩ UT MINISTRI OMNES AD MISSAM COMMUNICENT.

Anacletus papa omnibus Christi sacerdotibus. Peracta autem consecratione omnes communicent ... ecclesia et si hoc neglexerint degradetur.

(Burchard 3.77, PL 140.690, MC 45, p. 125, MC 44, p. 106)

⟨CCCXXXI⟩ DE ECCLESIIS DESTRUCTIS QUOMODO RESTAURARI DEBEANT.

Ygynus papa episcopis omnibus. Ecclesie destructe ubi aut plures sunt ...
p. 199 / ... providentia modis inveniatur qualiter consistere possit.

(Burchard 3.21, PL 140.676, MC 45, p. 113, MC 44, p. 98)

⟨CCCXXXII⟩ DE EODEM RE.

Gregorius servus servorum dei Iohanni Ravennanti episcopo. Placuit ut loca iamdudum consecrata et nunc ... iuxta possibilitatem in antiquum statum reformentur.

(Burchard 3.16, PL 140.676, MC 45, p. 112, MC 44, p. 98)

⟨CCCXXXIII⟩ DE EODEM RE.

Vigilius papa Eutero episcopo. De fabrica cuiuslibet ecclesie si dirupta
p. 200 fuerit ... / ... et missarum sollempnitate reverentiam sanctificationis accipiet.

(Burchard 3.62, PL 140.686, MC 45, p. 122, MC 44, p. 104)

⟨CCCXXXIV⟩ UT NULLUS ALIUD ALTARE PRESUMAT NISI AB EPISCOPO CONSECRATUM EST.

Hormisda papa universis Christi sacerdotibus. Statuimus ut nullus presbi-
p. 201 ter in ecclesia consecrata ... / ... si clericus est degradetur, si laicus anathematizetur.

(Burchard 3.17, PL 140.676, MC 45, p. 112, MC 44, p. 98)

⟨CCCXXXV⟩ Ex concilio Eparinensi.

Altaria si non sunt lapidea chrismatis unctione non consecrentur.

Burchard 3.25, PL 140.677, MC 45, p. 113, MC 44, p. 99)

⟨CCCXXXVI⟩ De lignis dedicate ecclesie ad quas usu verti debeant.

Ygynus papa episcopis omnibus. Ligna ecclesie dedicate non debent aliud opus ... in laicorum opera non debent admitti.

(Burchard 3.39, PL 140.679, MC 45, p. 115, MC 44, p. 100)

⟨CCCXXXVII⟩ De presbiteris qui missas solus (*sic*) soli celebrare.

Soter papa universis episcopis. Statutum est ut nullus presbitorum missarum sollempnia celebrare presumat nisi duobus presentibus sibique respondentibus ipse tertius habeatur.

(Burchard 3.74, PL 140.689, MC 45, p. 125, MC 44, p. 106)

. 202 ⟨CCCXXXVIII⟩ De consuetudine servanda que non est contra fidem. /

Pius Romane urbis archiepiscopus ecclesiis omnibus. Petistis enim per Hylarium cartularium nostrum a beate memorie decessore nostro ut omnes vobis retro ... contra fidem catholicam nichil usurpare dinoscitur.

(Burchard 3.124, PL 140.696, MC 45, p. 131, MC 44, p. 120)

⟨CCCXXXIX⟩ Quod non oporteat clericum aliqua spectacula interesse.

Martinus papa episcopis omnibus. Non liceat sacerdotibus vel clericis aliqua spectacula ... ipsa spectacula surgere et redire inde.

(Burchard 2.135, PL 140.648, MC 45, p. 88, MC 44, p. 80)

. 203 ⟨CCCXL⟩ Ut ante horam diei tertiam non sint misse celebrande /

Thelesphorus papa omnibus episcopis. Missarum celebrationes ante horam diei tertiam ... descendisse legitur excepta noctem sancte nativitatis.

(Burchard 3.63, PL 140.686, MC 45, p. 122, MC 44, p. 104)

⟨CCCXLI⟩ DE EPISCOPO QUI EGRITUDINEM AD SYNODUM VENIRE NON POTUERIT.

Felix alme Rome ecclesie episcopus episcopis omnibus. Quam si egrotans fuerit episcopus aut aliqua ... salva fidei veritate quicquid synodus statuerit.

(Burchard 1.51, PL 140.563, MC 45, p. 18, MC 44, p. 21)

⟨CCCXLII⟩ DE ILLIS EPISCOPIS QUI SUPERBIRE INCIPIUNT.

Gregorius episcopus servis servorum dei universis episcopis. Humilis de-
p. 204 bet esse episcopus, gradum enim mansuetudinis ... mansuetum esse /
non elatum non superbum.

(Burchard 1.14, PL 140.553, MC 45, p. 11, MC 44, p. 13)

⟨CCCXLIII⟩ DE EPISCOPO QUI IN SUA FUERIT PERSECUTUS ECCLESIA QUOD AD ALIA SIT FUGIENDUM.

Calixtus papa episcopis per Galliam constitutis. Si quis episcopus persecutus in sua fuerit ecclesia ... in una civitate fugite in aliam.

(Burchard 1.80, PL 140.570, MC 45, p. 23, MC 44, p. 27)

⟨CCCXLIV⟩ DE DEGRADATIS SACERDOTIBUS.

Celestinus papa omnibus episcopis. Sacerdos depositus in tali loco constituatur ubi peccata iugeat et ulterius non commitate.

(5L 2.87, Forn. 232, C. p. 91)

⟨CCCXLV⟩ SI PRO NECESSITATE IN VINO BAPTIZATUR EGROTUS.

Syricius papa catholicis omnibus. Qui in vino pro necessitate baptizat ...
p. 205 / ... permaneat, similiter quod in qualicumque liquore.

(5L 3.37, Forn. 331, C. p. 124)

⟨CCCXLVI⟩ DE BAPTISMATIS LINIRE CHRISMA PRESBITERI.

Silvester papa in generali residens synodo dixit: Statuimus ut baptizatum liniat presbiter chrismate levatum de aqua propter occasionem transitus mortis.

(5L 3.45, Forn. 333, C. p. 126)

⟨CCCXLVII⟩ DE CHRISMATE IN FRONTIBUS.

Gregorius Ianuario episcopo Caralitano. Audivimus quosdam scandalizatos quod presbyteros tangere ... frontibus baptizandos chrismate tangere debeant concedimus.

(5L 3.26, Forn. 326, C. p. 127)

⟨CCCXLVIII⟩ DE SACERDOTE QUI BAPTISMUM DENEGAVERINT.

p. 206 Gregorius. Si quis sacerdos baptismum cuiquam in periculo ... / ... et luctu inter laicos penitentia se subdat. Si quis baptismum abnegaverit, episcopus et presbiter reus erit animarum.

(cf. 5L 3.35, Forn. 330, and 5L, 3.46.3, Forn. 334; and cf. 5L 3.28c, b, C. p. 128)

⟨CCCXLIX⟩ QUOD IN SABBATO VACATIO FIERI NON DEBET.

GREGORIUS.

Gregorius civibus Romane. Pervenit ad nos quasdam perverse mentis ... dominicum ab omni faciet custodiri opere.

(5L 3.63, Forn. 343, C. p. 132)

⟨CCCL⟩ DE OBSERVATIONE DOMINICI DIEI.

Eugenius papa omnibus christianis. Constat omnino observari ut die do-
p. 207 minico ... / ... vocabulo nuncupatur convenenter (*sic*) opera agere videantur.

(5L 3.54.1, Forn. 339, C. p. 130)

⟨CCCLI⟩ QUOD TRICENNALIS POSSESSIO FIT INTACTA PERMANSIT MILITARI NON DEBET.

Gelasius ecclesiis omnibus. Illud etiam annecti placuit ut si quod absit facultates ecclesie ... pro eo appellare quod legum tempus excludit.

(Burchard 3.149, PL 140.702, MC 45, p. 136, MC 44, p. 113)

⟨CCCLII⟩ QUOD NULLI LICEAT CONCUBINAM ET UXOREM HABERE.

Eugenius papa omnibus christianis. Sicut nulli licet uno tempore duas
p. 208 habere uxores ... / ... ita viri castum debent custodire coniugum.

(5L 5.28c, C. p. 278)

⟨CCCLIII⟩ DE CUPIENDO VEL FUGIENDO HONORE.

Gregorius episcopus Cyriaco episcopo. Sicut locus regiminis desiderantibus negandus est ... si vocatur a deo tanquam Aaron.

(5L 1.39, Forn. 39, C. p. 16)

⟨CCCLIV⟩ DE SACERDOTIBUS LAPSIS.

Gregorius Ianuario episcopo Caralitano. Pervenit ad nos quosdam de sa-
p. 209 cris ordinibus lapsos ... / ... aut permanere aut revocare posse cognoscas.

(5L 2.96, 98, Forn. 236, 237; cf 5L 2.53d and 54, C. p. 92)

⟨CCCLV⟩ UT MULIERES IN MONASTERIUM VIRORUM INGREDI DEBEANT NEC EAS COMMATRES MONACHI PRESUMANT.

p. 210 Gregorius Valentino abbati. Pervenit ad nos quod in monasterium ... / ... tue qualitate ceteris sine dubio corrigantur.

(5L 2.195, Forn. 291, C. p. 117; and cf. MC 522, p. 209)

⟨CCCLVI⟩ DE RESTITUTIONE DEPOSITI.

Clemens papa omnibus presbiteris. Super omnia autem avaritiam fugite que homines ... quibusque equissima custodite, deposita fideliter restituite.

(5L 4.121a, b[rubr.], C. 232)

⟨CCCLVII⟩ DE EODEM RE.

Si accepisti commendatum observa ne perdideris si perdideris reddes neglegentiam.

(5L 4.119b, C. p. 231, attributed to Origen)

⟨CCCLVIII⟩ ITEM.

IERONIMUS.

Quicumque amiserit per neglegentiam commendatum proximi sui reddat quantum perdidit.

(5L 4.119b, C. p. 231)

AUGUSTINUS.

Noli neglegere commendatum proximi, ne coram iudice damno reddas quod neglexeris.

(5L 4.119b, C. p. 231)

p. 211 ⟨CCCLIX⟩ ITEM SYNODUS AMBIENENSIS /

Si quis clericorum depositum accepit et per furtum ... ut non reddatur, non est accipiendum.

(5L 4.120, C. p. 232)

⟨CCCLX⟩ DE HIS QUI MATRIMONIO SUNT IUNCTI ET COMCUMBERE NON POSSUNT.

Gregorius episcopus Iohanni Ravennati episcopo. Quod autem interro-
p. 212 gasti de his qui matrimoniis ... / ... si autem ille aliam acceperit seper-
arentur (*sic*).

(Burchard 9.40, PL 140.821, MC 45, p. 237, MC 44, p. 177; cf. MC 522, p. 188)

⟨CCCLXI⟩ QUID AGENDUM SIT SI EVENERIT FAMES, PESTILENTIA, VEL EQUALITAS AERIS.

Liberius papa omnibus christianis. Constituimus quod si evenerit fames, pestilentia ... elemosinis et observationibus (*sic*) domini misericordia deprecetur.

(Burchard 13.18, PL 140.888, MC 45, p. 280, MC 44, p. 212)

⟨CCCLXII⟩ DE ILLIS QUI PACEM RECUSANT.

Fabianus papa universis catholicis. Si quis contristatus noluerit reconciliari satisfaciente ... usque dum gratanti animo satisfactionem recipiat.

(Burchard 10.59, PL 140.852, MC 45, p. 263, MC 44, p. 193)

⟨CCCLXIII⟩ UT EPISCOPI POSTERIORES SE PRIORIBUS SUIS NON PREFERANT.

Lucius papa omnibus episcopis occidentalibus. Episcopi per singulas pro-
p. 213 vincias observent ne posteriores ... / ... ad propriam pertinet parrochiam aliquid agant.

(Burchard 1.54, PL 140.563, MC 45, p. 19, MC 44, p. 22)

⟨CCCLXIV⟩ DE REBUS DUBIIS IN CONCILIIS EPISCOPORUM EMERGENTIBUS.

Bonifatius papa episcopis Gallie. Si inter episcopos eiusdem concilii dubitatio ... nulla pars valeat calculo eius contradicere.

(Burchard 1.57, PL 140.564, MC 45, p. 19, MC 44, p. 22)

⟨CCCLXV⟩ DE QUATTUOR MODIS QUIBUS VIVI ADIUVANT MORTUOS.

Gregorius omnibus christianis. Anime defunctorum quattuor modis solu-
p. 214 untur: oblationibus presbiterorum, preces / sanctorum, carorum helemosinis, ieiuniis cognatorum.

(5L 3.319.2, Forn. 481, attributed to Origen, C. p. 178, attributed to Gregory; Burchard 19.112, PL 140.1006, attributed to Origen, MC 44, p. 278)

⟨CCCLXVI⟩ SI DEBEANT DUO FRATRES GERMANI SINGULAS SORORES ACCIPERE.

Gregorius Augustino episcopo Anglorum. Interrogastis si debeant duo fratres germani ... ex tali coniugio soboles non posse succrescere.

(Ps.-Isidore, Hinschius pp. 738 f.; cf. Burchard 7.19, PL 140.782, and Ivo, Dec. 9.55, PL 161.669, and Pan. 7.71, PL 161.1299)

⟨CCCLXVII⟩ DE ANIMABUS PARVULORUM.

Gregorius Secundino. In extremo epistole requisisti quid ei responden-
p. 215 dum ... / ... questio nec valet ab homine comprehendi.

(MC 522, p. 216; cf. Gregory, Reg. 9.148; CCSL 140A.703)

⟨CCCLXVIII⟩ QUICQUID COMMOTUS ANIMO FACERE HOC IUSTUM PUTAT.

Gregorius episcopus Mauricio imperatori. Omnipotenti deo reus est qui
p. 216 serenissimo domino ... / ... nam commotionis tempore iustum putat ira
quod fecit.

(Burchard 15.29, PL 140.902, MC 45, p. 299, MC 44, p. 221)

⟨CCCLXIX⟩ DE QUERENTIBUS MUTARI LOCUM.

Gregorius omnibus monachis. Sepe cum querimus mutari locum cona-
p. 217 mur ... / ... potuisset satanas de celo non cecidisset.

(5L 3.172.1, Forn. 395, C. p. 148)

⟨CCCLXX⟩ DE CORONA CLERICORUM.

Anicius papa episcopis omnibus. Prohibete fratres per universas regionum vestrarum ... et omni habitu discreti debent apparere.

(MC 1, p. 58; Hinschius, p. 122; cf. Ivo, Dec. 6.46, PL 161.454)

⟨CCCLXXI⟩ DE EO QUOD SANCTI APOSTOLI EORUMQUE SUCCESSORES VOLUERINT DIFFICILEM ESSE ACCUSATIONEM SACERDOTUM.

Fabianus papa episcopis orientalibus. Talia cogitantes sancti apostoli eo-
p. 218 rumque successores ... / ... propriis sedibus aut ecclesiis episcopi eiceren-
tur (*sic*).

(Burchard 1.183, PL 140.603, MC 45, p. 50, MC 44, p. 51)

⟨CCCLXXII⟩ QUID AGENDUM SIT IN CAUSIS DE QUIBUS CERTA IN CANONIBUS NON INVENIUNT IUDICIUM.

p. 219 Innocentius papa Decentio episcopo. De quibus / causis nulla solvendi
p. 220 ligandique ... petierint fiet illis / a patre meo.

(Ivo, Dec. 4.70, PL 161.283)

⟨CCCLXXIII⟩ QUOD NUSQUAM CANONES PRECIPIANT UT PER EGRITUDINEM ALIUS SUCCEDAT ET SIPSE (*sic*) PRO SUA MOLESTIA PETIERIT QUALITER FIERI POSSIT.

Gregorius Anatolio diacono. Scripsit mihi dilectio tua me reverentissimo
fratri meo Iohanni prime Iustiniane episcopo pro egritudine capitis quam
p. 221 patitur episcopum ... / ... offendatur neque civitas neglecta esse inveni-
atur.

(Burchard 1.188, PL 140.604, MC 45, p. 50, MC 44, p. 52; cf. 5L 1.160, Forn. 108, C. p. 45, and MC 522, p. 221)

⟨CCCLXXIV⟩ UT EGROTO EPISCOPO ORDINARI SUCCESSORES POSSIT.

Gregorius Mariniano episcopo Ravennati. Qualiter ordinati a nobis sacer-
p. 222 dotes corporis ... / ... et idem a nobis disponente deo consecretur antistis.

(cf. Burchard 1.189, PL 140.605, MC 45, p. 50, MC 44, p. 52; and MC 522, p. 215)

⟨CCCLXXV⟩ UT PUERI AD SACRUM ORDINEM NON AMMITTANTUR.

Gregorius Columbano episcopo. Itaque erga primates synodi tu esto ... venalitas nec potentia vel supplicatio personarum.

(5L 1.76, Forn. 64, C. p. 28)

⟨CCCLXXVI⟩ QUOD QUI SEMEL ORDINATUS EST ITERUM ORDINARI NON DEBEAT.

Gregorius Iohanni Ravennati episcopo. Absit a fraternitate vestra sic sa-
p. 223 pere ... / ... pro culpa penitentia indici debet et tamen ordo servari.

(5L 1.78, Forn. 65, C. p. 28; and cf. MC 522, p. 203)

⟨CCCLXXVII⟩ DE SACRAMENTO APUD TIMENTES DEUM.

Gregorius Mariniano episcopo. Si qua forte causa inter ecclesiam et monasterium ... voluntaria cadulatione (*sic*) mediis sacrosanctis evangeliis firmatur.

(5L 4.142d, C. p. 238)

⟨CCCLXXVIII⟩ QUOD POTEST MULIER ENIXA EADEM DIE ECCLESIAM INTRARE SIMILITER ET MENSTRUA.

Gregorius Augustino episcopo Anglorum. Interrogasti cum enixa fuerit
p. 224 mulier post quot dies ... / ... superfluitas in culpam non debet computari.

(cf. 5L 5.88, C. p. 312)

[The remainder of the page has been erased and a reagent used to bring up a prayer copied in red and black, which is now almost totally illegible]

ORATIO SANCTI AUGUSTINI EPISCOPI.

... patris advenisti ut nos ... redimeres quia scio et ... non propter iustos sed propter peccatores ... terra ... voluisti. Ex ... domine ... peccatorem et culpabilem ....

(cf. Alcuin, De psalmorum usu, Oratio VI. Pro custodienda humilitate et cognitione humanae fragilitatis, PL 101.476)

Incipits

Ab infirmis in periculo mortis positis CXCV
Absit a fraternitate vestra sic sapere CCCLXXVI
Accusandi vel testificandi licentia denegetur his CCCXV
Accusatores et testes esse non possunt CCCXVI
Agamus hos dies cum summa reverentia CCXLII
Agnovimus penitentiam morientibus denegari nec illorum CCCXXV
Aliorum hominum causas deus voluit discussoris CCCIV
Altaria si non sunt lapidea chrismatis CCCXXXV
Anacletus servus Christi Iesu et ceteris cunctis fidelibus. Qui abstulerit patri vel matri aliquid CCXXXI
Animalia coytu hominum polluta occidantur carnesque LXXIV
Anime defunctorum quattuor modis soluuntur: oblationibus presbiterorum CCCLXV
Audivimus quosdam scandalizatos quod presbyteros tangere CCCXLVII

Caveat ante omnia sacerdos ne de ius VII
Centum soleri dati in elemosinam unum annum CCXCVIII
Clerici inter epulas cantantes ab officio CCXLV
Clericis sine commendaticiis litteris episcopi sui CCLXX
Clericos scurriles et verbis turpibus ioculatores CCXXXVI
Clericus fideiussionibus inserviens abiciatur CCXXXIV
Clericus invidens fratrum provectionibus donec in vitio CCLII
Clericus nec comam nutriat nec barbam CCXLVII
Clericus qui adulationibus et proditionibus vacare CCXLVIII
Clericus qui intra muros civitates manet CCXLIII
Clericus si semen fuderit non tangendo LVIII
Concubuisti cum uxore tua die dominico CI
Concubuisti cum uxore tua post manifestam conceptionem CVIII
Concubuisti cum uxore tua postquam infans CVIII
Constat omnino observari ut die dominico CCCL
Constituimus quod si evenerit fames, pestilentia CCCLXI
Corporale super quod sacra oblatio immolatur CCLXVII
Corrupisti virginem et postea eadem dixisti CI
Cotidie eucharistie communionem accipere nec laudo CLXXVI
Cuius parvulus per neglegentiam sine baptisimo CCLXXVI

Curandum vero maxime et omni cautela IX

De fabrica cuiuslibet ecclesie si dirupta fuerit CCCXXXIII
De eo quod interrogastis si ille CCXXIII
De eo qui in baptismate quacumque CCLXXVIII
De his etiam requisivit dilectio tua CCXXI
De his qui irrationabiliter versati sunt LXXIII
De his qui se incesti pollutionem LXIV
De quibus causis nulla solvendi ligandique CCCLXXIII
De raptoribus autem feminarum id constituendum esse censuimus, ut si ad ecclesiam CCLXII
Decimas quas in usum pietatis concessas CCXXXII
Decretum est in eodem concilio ut presbiter aliquis post gallicantum CCVII
Definitio incauta laudabiliter solvenda non prevaricatione CXXXIV
Dictum etiam nobis est quasdam feminas CCXXII
Duodecim triduane singule cum psalteriis tribus CCXCV

E contra qui non dei sancteque ecclesie contemptor CCLIX
Ecclesia que ab adulteriis contaminata fuerit CCLVI
Ecclesie destructe ubi aut plures sunt CCCXXXI
Eos qui ad ecclesiam confugerit tradi CCLVII
Episcopi et presbiteri examinent qualiter confitentium III
Episcopi per singulas provincias observent ne posteriores CCCLXIII
Episcopus aut presbiter dum ingressus fuerit CCVI
Episcopus, presbiter, aut diaconus alee atque ebrietati CLXXXV
Episcopus, presbiter aut diaconus usuras a debitoribus CCXLIX
Episcopus, presbiter, aut diaconus si a gradu suo iniuste CCLXXV
Est in eadem illusionem necessaria valde CLXXV
Et de rebus ecclesiarum que ab eis CCLXXXI
Et hoc quoque statutum est ut relictam CCXVIII
Eucharistia cotidie te cibum salutis accipit CLXXVIII
Exercuisti lenocinium aut in te ipsa CVIII

Falsas penitentias dicimus que non secundum auctoritatem CXCIII
Fecisti fornicationem ut quidam facere solent ita dico LXI
Fecisti fornicationem ut quidam facere solent tu tuum virile membrum LX
Fecisti periurium coactus et per necessitatem CXXXI
Fecisti periurium per cupiditatem xl. dies CXXIX
Fecisti periuriam sciens et alios in periurium CXXX
Fecisti solus tecum fornicationesm, ut quidam LIX
Fecisti truncationem manuum aut pedum aut oculos XXXVI
Fuisti in falso testimonio ita dico CXL

Grave nimis et contra sacerdotale constat CCCVI

Habet sacrosancta Romana ecclesia potestatem singulari CCCIII
His qui in tempore necessitatis et in periculi CCII
Honestum nobis et iustum videtur ut CXXIV
Humilis debet esse episcopus, gradum enim mansuetudinis CCCXLII

Iis qui vivente marito coniugem illius CCXXV
Illud etiam annecti placuit ut si quod absit facultates ecclesie CCCLI
Illud quod per complemento communionis quidam intinctam CCIII
In cena domini a quibusdam perceptio eucharistie CLXXX
In concilio Antioceno simul et in Calcedonensi precipitur, ut fugitivi clerici et peregrini CCLXIX
In extremo epistole requisisti quid ei respondendum CCCLXVII
In tabulis vel codicibus sorte futura CXCI
Infames esse personas dicimus que per aliqua culpa CCCXVIII
Institutio illa sancta que fiebat in diebus I
Interdixit per omnia magna synodus non episcopo non presbitero CXV
Interrogasti cum enixa fuerit mulier post quot dies CCCLXXVIII
Interrogastis si debeant duo fratres germani CCCLXVI
Iste annus secundus est ab illo anno CCXCIX
Ita ergo necessitatibus talium auxiliandum est CCII
Itaque erga primates synodi tu esto CCCLXXVI
Iuramentum filii aut filie nesciente parte CXXV

Laicus si per ebrietatem vomitum facit CLXXXIII
Ligna ecclesie dedicate non debent aliud opus CCCXXXVI
Loca humandi corporis pretio non possunt adipisci CCC

Manifesta peccata non sunt occulta correctione VIII
Mechatus es cum uxore alterius tu non habens uxorem CX
Melior est penitentia brevis cum fervore XII
Missarum celebrationes ante horam diei tertiam CCCXL
Molles id es *sic*, effeminati qui super se feminas LXXXIV
Monachi procreantes filios in carcere secludanturCXIX
Monachus si uxorem accipiat tantum in finem CIX
Mulier enixa si vult communionem percipiat CLXXXI
Mulier que aut laborat ut non concipiat XLVIII
Mulier quocumque molimine aut in se LXX
Mulier si cum muliere fornicata fuerit LXXII
Mulier si divinationes vel incantationes diabolicas CXC

Nemo clericus vel diaconus vel presbiter propter quamlibet causam CCCXX
Nemo iudicavit primam sedem iustitiam temperari CCCII
Nemo presbiter vel diaconus a die honoris presbiteri CXIV
Nemo presbiterorum xenium vel quodcumque emolumentum V

Noli neglegere commendatum proximi, ne coram iudice CCCLVIII
Non debet episcopus aut presbiter aut diaconus commisceri CXCVIII
Non est publice confitendum peccatum sed absconse VI
Non liceat abbas filios de baptismo suscipere CCLXXXV
Non liceat sacerdotibus vel clericis aliqua spectacula CCCXXXIX
Non oportet clericos vel laicos religiosos ante sacram horam diei CCLXXI
Non oportet filiam de sacro fonte CXX
Nosse desideras utrum mulier que viri CCXXIX
Nulla mulier potionem accipiat ut non concipiat XLIX
Nullas potiones diabolicas debent mulieres accipere L
Nulli liceat ignorare omne quod domino CLIII
Nulli quoque penitentiam ex corde suo III
Nulli sacerdotum liceat suos canones ignorare II
Nullus aut viduam aut filiam extra parentum CCXVI
Nullus episcopus, presbiter, diaconus aut subdiaconus ad secretum CXVI
Nullus proprium filium aut filiam a fonte baptismatisCCXXIV
Nullus sacerdotum causam suam alieno committat CCCXXI

Observandum est, ut mensa Christi, id est altare ubi corpus CCLXVI
Omne depositum redditur nisi depositum ecclesie CCLXXXVII
Omnes basilice cum missa debent semper consecrari CCCXXIX
Omnia que deo offeruntur consecrata habeantur CCX
Omnipotenti deo reus est qui serenissimo domino CCCLXVIII
Omnis decime terre sive de frugibus sive de pomis CCXI

Penitentia illius anni talis esse debet CCXCIX
Penitentia unius anni qui in pane CCXCIX
Penitentibus secundum differentiam peccatorum sacerdotis arbitrio XI
Per huius nostri apostolici privilegii sancimus, ut loca que prephato beati Benedicti monasterio concessa sunt CCCXI
Per singulos menses gravia atque torpentia CCXXXI
Peracta autem consecratione omnes communicent CCCXXX
Pervenit ad conscientiam apostolice sedis quod nonnulli CCCXXII
Pervenit ad nos quasdam perverse mentis CCCXLIX
Pervenit ad nos quod in monasterium CCCLV
Pervenit ad nos quosdam de sacris ordinibus CCCLIV
Petistis enim per Hylarium cartularium nostrum a beate memorie decessore nostro ut omnes vobis retro CCCXXXVIII
Placuit nobis ut letania maior observanda sit a cunctis CCXLI
Placuit ut loca iamdudum consecrata et nunc CCCXXXII
Placuit sancto et magno Calcedonensi concilio dcxxx. sacerdotes sub Marciano principe affuerunt ut si quis vir uxorem XXXIX
Ponunt canones peccantibus de quibusdam peccatis CCXCI
Postulastis a nobis quatinus concederemus et confirmaremus CCCXIV

Posuisti infantem tuum iuxta ignem et alius XLVII
Presbiter aut diaconus qui in fornicatione CXXII
Presbiter vel diaconus vel subdiaconus vel quilibet ecclesie deputatus clericus CCXLIII
Presbiterorum filios a sacri altaris ministeriis CCVIII
Presbiterum in nuptiis bigami prandere non convenit CCLXXIII
Privilegia ecclesiarum et monasteriorum intemerata et CCCV
Privilegia ecclesiarum et monasteriorum sanctorum patrum CCCVI
Pro reverentia dei et sacerdotum id universa sancta synodus statuit ut quia solent crebra mensis otiose CCXXXV
Pro uno die quem in pane et aqua CCXCII
Procul dubio hii qui eos persequuntur CCCXXIII
Prohibete fratres per universas regionum vestrarum CCCLXX
Pueri qui fornicationem inter semetipsos iudicium LXIII

Quacumque arte verborum quisque iuret deus CXXXV
Qualiter ordinati a nobis sacerdotes corporis CCCLXXIV
Quam si egrotans fuerit episcopus aut aliqua CCCXLI
Quam sit necessarium monasteriorum quieti prospicere CCCVIII
Quemadmodum antecessores nostri eorum privilegiis antecessoribus CCCXIII
Qui abstulerit patri vel matri aliquid CCXXXI
Qui acceperit sacrificium post cibum aut CLXXI
Qui auguria, auspicia sive somnia vel divinationes CLXXXVII
Qui autem psalmos nescit per uno die CCXCIV
Qui compulsus a domino periurans se CXXXII
Qui consenserit inscius ad falsum testimonium antequam studeas CXXXVII
Qui episcopum occiderit secundum antiquam diffinitionem XIII
Qui euchastiam *sic*, in ecclesiam accipiat CLXXVII
Qui fratribus suis falso capitalia obiecisse CXXXVIII
Qui ieiunare non potest et non habet CCXCIII
Qui in quadragesima ante pascha cognoverit XCIII
Qui in vino pro necessitate baptizat CCCXLV
Qui oblationes defunctorum aut negant ecclesiis CCIX
Qui odii meditatione vel propter cupiditatem XX
Qui operatur die dominico septum dies peniteat CCLXXX
Qui ordinatus episcopus aut presbiter aut diaconus CXVII
Qui per ebrietatem vomitum facit, si presbiter CLXXXII
Qui per illecebroso amplexus femine vel osculo LVII
Qui per rixam et ictum debilem XXXVII
Qui per turpiloquium illud apostoli preceptum LVI
Qui periurat in manu episcopi aut in cruce CXXIV
Qui rapiunt puellas aut mulieres auctores CIV
Qui sacramento se obligaverit ut litiget CXLIII

Qui venerit in secundas nuptias penitentia LXXXIX
Qui verba acerbiora in furore non CXLVI
Quia dies sabbati tempore sanctos patres nostros CXCIV
Quicumque amiserit per neglegentiam commendatum proximi sui CCCLVIII
Quicumque filios procreaverit causa pesteritatis nutrire LI
Quicumque furtivum comederit erit et sciat CLXIII
Quicumque iudex aut secularis presbitero CCXXXVIII
Quicumque operator fuerit carnalis copule nutriendi LII
Quicumque presbiter de iure tituli sui CLV
Quicumque res naufragorum diripiunt ut raptores CCCXXVII
Quod autem interrogasti de his qui matrimoniis CCCLX
Quod non oporteat a septuagesima usque in octavis pasche CCXII
Quod oporteat eos qui baptizantur post lavacrum CCLXXVII
Quod si quis dei sancteque ecclesie extiterit CCLIX
Quod si vir non habens uxorem LXXXVIII
Quoniam sunt quidam qui die dominico CCXL
Quotiens cumque a sede apostolica aliqua CCCIX

Rimande sunt accusatorum enucleatim persone qui CCCXIX
Raptor publica penitentia multetur, raptam vero CCXVII
Rationis ordo non patitur ut monasterium CCCVII
Relatum est auribus sanctorum sacerdotum quidam ulterius uxorem CCXXVI
Reum confugientem ad ecclesiam sue in atrium CCLVIII

Sacerdos depositus in tali loco constituatur CCCXLIV
Sacrilegi sunt ecclesiarum predones unde in concilio Agathensi CLI
Sacrilegium id est sacrorum rerum furtum CL
Sacrosancta Romana et apostolica ecclesia non ab apostolis CCCI
Sancitum est atque omnibus modis prohibitum ut siquis presbiter inventum fuerit CCLXIII
Sancta synodus cl. patrum sub Theodosio seniore Constantinopolim congregata pro plerosque implices minusque capaces hoc strictim breviterque XVI
Sanctorum patrum sententiis consona consentientes ex dei CCIV
Sanctus Ambrosius dixit: Si quotiens cumque effunditur sanguinis Christi CLXXVIIIb
Sanctus Cyprianus dixit: Eucharistia cotidie te cibum salutis accipitur CLXXVIIIa
Sanctus Hylarius episcopus dixit: Si non tanta sunt peccata ut CLXXVIIIc
Sane quisquis positus in ultima necessitate CXCVI
Scripsit mihi dilectio tua me reverentissimo fratri meo Iohanni prime Iustiniane episcopo pro egritudine capitis quam patitur episcopum CCCLXXIII
Seculares vero qui in natalis domini CCXLIV

Seditionarios nunquam ordinandos clericos sicut nec usurarios CCLIII
Sepe cum querimus mutari locum conamur CCCLXIX
Septuaginta quinque psalmi cum cotidem veniis CCXCVII
Sex genera sunt nolentia homocidiorum primum XVIII
Si accepisti commendatum observa ne perdideris CCCLVII
Si aliquis de ministerio ecclesie quolibet modo CLX
Si aliquis manducat aut bibit aut portat CLXXXIX
Si conscio marito et ipsa consentiente LXXXVII
Si cuius parvulus per neglegentiam sine chrismate CCLXXIX
Si cum masculo inter coxas ut quidam LXII
Si devota peccaverit vel se maritaverit XCIX
Si expositis ante ecclesiam cuiusque fuerit miseratione CCLXI
Si fur aut latro captus in preda XXV
Si homo fornicatus fuerit cum muliere CCI
Si inter episcopos eiusdem concilii dubitatio CCCLXIV
Si laicus cum femina laica, id est uterque LXXXVI
Si libera mulier publicum servum sibi copulaverit C
Si mater filium suum sponte occiderit XLI
Si mechatus es tu uxoratus cum alterius uxore CXI
Si motum fuerit altare denuo consecretur ecclesia CCCXXVIII
Si mulier se vivum vel sanum XLIII
Si non tanta sunt peccata ut CLXXVIIIc
Si osculatus est episcopus per desiderium LXXV
Si pater scienter et voluntarie necat XL
Si per cogitationem semen episcopus effuderit LV
Si per negligentiam de calice aliquid CLXVIII
Si plures heredes contenderint de communi ecclesia CCLXV
Si post illusionem que per sompnum CLXXIV
Si qua domina furore zeli accensa XXIII
Si qua femina in fornicatione deprehensa XCVII
Si qua fidelis mulier oppresserit per negligentiam XLIV
Si qua forte causa inter ecclesiam et monasterium CCCLXXVII
Si qua mulier fornicaverit et infantem XLVI
Si qua mulier invenerit iuxta se XLII
Si qua mulier posteri viri amore capto CVI
Si qua mulier posuerit infantem suum XLII
Si qua mulier virum proprium relinquens CCLXXIV
Si qua puella desponsata alterius et postea rapta CIII
Si quis a medicis per languorem LIV
Si quis a se vel a parentibus CCLXXXIV
Si quis abbas rem mobilem sive immobilem CLVI
Si quis acceperit eius qui captivatus est CV
Si quis ad mercedem ieiunaverit si per ignorantiam CCXC

Si quis alium per iram percusserit XXXV
Si quis aream aut domum cuiusque CLVIII
Si quis castellum aut alicuius municipium XXXIII
Si quis castrum sponte incenderit per multa XXVIII
Si quis clericorum depositum accepit et per furtum CCCLIX
Si quis clericus aut laicus in demoliendis CLVII
Si quis clericus aut monachus furtum CLXVI
Si quis clericus aut monachus postquam deo XCI
Si quis clericus aut monachus verba scurrilia CCXLVI
Si quis coactus pro vita redimenda CXXVIII
Si quis commendavit pecuniam placuit ut accipiat CCLXXXVI
Si quis commovetur et tantum sentit CXLVII
Si quis conceptum mulieris deceperit si XLV
Si quis concupiscens fornicari etiam si eius XC
Si quis contra alium iram tenet CXLIV
Si quis contristatus noluerit reconciliari satisfaciente CCCLXII
Si quis cum deo sacrata vel uxore XCVI
Si quis cum ea quam propter deum XCVII
Si quis cum filia spirituali et ipsa XCV
Si quis cum matre et filia fornicatus CC
Si quis cum scorta adulterium sepe CXXI
Si quis cum sponsa alterius fornicaverit XCVIII
Si quis custodierit clavem domus et fur CCLXXXVIII
Si quis delator extiterit fidelis et XXX
Si quis diu amaritudinem retinet in corde CXLV
Si quis divinis tactis scripturis iuraverit CCXIX
Si quis duas uxores habuerit aut uxorem CXII
Si quis dum divina misteria celebrantur CCLX
Si quis duxerit de propria cogitatione LXXX
Si quis ecclesiam dei per aliquam intentionem CLIV
Si quis ecclesiam igne comburit quindecim annos CLII
Si quis ecclesiastica preditus ordinatione aut monachus CLXXXV
Si quis ecclesie dei nequiter violator CCLIV
Si quis eorum qui continentie student CCLXXII
Si quis episcopum, presbiterum, vel diaconum aut aliquem exordinatis falsis criminibus CXXXIX
Si quis episcopus alicui detrahit quindecim dies CXLI
Si quis episcopus homicidium fecerit xv. XIV
Si quis episcopus persecutus in sua fuerit ecclesia CCCXLIII
Si quis episcopus, presbiter aut diaconus post diem CXVIII
Si quis episcopus, presbiter, diaconus etiam monachus qui uxorem habuit XCIV
Si quis episcopus, presbiter, sive diaconus vel quilibet ex ordine clericorum

CLXXXVI
Si quis eucharistiam causa neglegentie perdiderit CLXIX
Si quis falsum testimonium dixerit si episcopus CXXXVI
Si quis fidelis habens virginem uxorem cum Iudea vel gentili CI
Si quis fornicatus fuerit cum duabus sororibus LXXXIII
Si quis fornicatio ut sodomite fecerit LXVIII
Si quis fratrem contristat iuste vel iniuste CXLVIII
Si quis furtum capitale commiserit id est aurum CLXI
Si quis hodio *sic*, habens aliquem ita CXLII
Si quis homicidium consenserit faciendum et factum XXVII
Si quis homicidium in ecclesia aut XV
Si quis hominem gratis expoliaverit in via CLXV
Si quis homines publice penitentem interfecit XIX
Si quis ieiunare non potest pro uno anno CCXCII
Si quis in altare ubi reliquie CXXIII
Si quis in atrio ecclesie pugnam committit CCLV
Si quis in ecclesia fornicatur quod nimis LXXVIII
Si quis in manu episcopi vel presbiteri CXXVII
Si quis in nocte cogitaverit fantasias LVI
Si quis inscius se periuraverit et postea CXXXIII
Si quis invitus aut coactus qualibet causa CXXVI
Si quis laicus alterum laicum pro rixas XVII
Si quis laicus concubinam habere antequam uxorem CXIII
Si quis laicus non habens uxorem LXXIX
Si quis mathematicus fuerit et per invocationem CLXXXVIII
Si quis mendacium fecerit per ignorantiam CXLIX
Si quis menstruo tempore coierit cum muliere CI
Si quis monasteria et loca deo CLIX
Si quis naufragios post maris evasionem CCLXXXIII
Si quis neglexerit sacrificium aut perdiderit CLXVII
Si quis Normannorum vel quorumlibet hominum predia monasteria beati Benedicti montis Casinensis invaserit vel quascumque CCCXIII
Si quis ordinatus in scelere sodomitico LXVI
Si quis oblata deo dederit vel acceperit CCXXXI
Si quis penitentiam alicui in periculo posito X
Si quis per maleficia aliquem hominem XXXI
Si quis per necessitatem furtatus fuerit CLXII
Si quis per nequitiam alium inebriat CLXXXIV
Si quis per qualecumque maleficium interfecit XXXII
Si quis per semetipsum quacumque ingenio fornicaveritLXVII
Si quis pontifex faciens facilem fornicationem LXXXIV
Si quis prebet ducatum barbaris si tredecim annos peniteat XXIX

Si quis precantaverint ad fascinum vel CXCII
Si quis presbiter penitentiam abnegaverit morientibus CCCXXIV
Si quis presbiteram duxerit in coniugium CCLXXXIX
Si quis presbiterum inhonorat aut verbo CCXXXIX
Si quis pro aqua vinum vino CLXXIII
Si quis quod est mercatus incestuosissimum CII
Si quis quolibet membrum precipue tamen virilia LIII
Si quis sacerdos baptismum cuiquam in periculo CCCXLVIII
Si quis sacerdos cum filia spirituali fornicatus CXCIX
Si quis sacerdos enormitatem post solitum cibum CLXXII
Si quis sacerdos sine cogitatione pollutus LVI
Si quis sacrificium vomuerit xl. dies CLXX
Si quis secularium pro calumpma ecclesiam CCXXXVII
Si quis servum aut quecumque hominem XXXIV
Si quis servum proprium sine conscientia XXI
Si quis servus dominum suum voluntarie occiderit XXII
Si quis super patrem suum vel matrem in iracundia XXXVIII
Si quis ultimo ad spectaculum mortis XXVI
Si quis uxorem suam invenerit adulteratam CVII
Si quis vexatur a demone et nescit XXIV
Si quis vir aut si qua mulier votum XCII
Si quis vir cum uxore sua retro nupserit LXIX
Si quotiens cumque effunditur CLXXVIII
Si rem alienam propter quam peccatum est CXCVII
Si sanctimonialis cum alia sanctimonialis per aliquod LXXI
Siscitatur a nobis sanctitas tua si aliquis CCXXVIII
Si semen per osculum fuderit episcopum iiii. annos peniteat LXXVI
Si semen per osculum fuderit episcopus i. annum peniteat LXXVII
Si tu abstines sine uxoris voluntate CCXX
Si unus ex coniugibus filium aut filiam alterius CCXXX
Si vult confiteri peccata sua sacerdoti CLXIV
Sicut laici et seculares homines volunt CCCXVIII
Sicut locus regiminis desiderantibus negandus est CCCLIII
Sicut nulli licet uno tempore duas habere uxores CCCLII
Singularum ecclesiarum rusticas parrochias vel possessiones CCLXXXII
Singulis dominicis diebus in quadragesima praeter illos CLXXIX
Solus Romanus pontifex universalis habetur teste Calcedonensi concilio CCXCIX
Sponsus et sponsa cum benedicendi sunt CCXIII
Statuimus ut baptizatum liniat presbiter chrismate levatum de aqua propter occasionem transitus mortis CCCXLVI
Statuimus ut ieiunia quattuor temporum hoc ordine CCCXXVI
Statuimus ut nullus presbiter in ecclesia consecrata CCCXXXIV

Statutum est ut nullus presbitorum missarum sollempnia celebrare CCCXXXVII
Sufficit sacerdoti unam missam in die una CCV
Sunt nonnullo fulti dogmate audacissime CCCX
Super omnia autem avaritiam fugite que homines CCCLVI
Synodus Romana statuit qui cum sua commatre LXXXII
Synodus statuit Romana: Monachi procreantes filios CXIX
Synodus Calcedonensis dcxxx. sacerdotum sub Marciano LXXXI

Talia cogitantes sancti apostoli eorumque successores CCCLXXI

Unusquisque presbiter capitula habeant de maioribus IV
Ut clericus si commendaverit pecuniam, pecuniam accipiat CCLI
Ut fugitivi clerici et peregrini CCLXIX
Ut laici secus altare quo sacra misteria CCLXVIII
Ut nullus fidelis cuiuscumque condicionis sit CCXIV
Ut nullus presbiter vel diaconus seu subdiaconus vel de qualicumque clericorum presumat legem CCXXXIII
Ut presbiteri a turpibus lucris et usuris non solum CCL
Ut quia solent crebra mensis otiose CCXXXV
Ut si quilibet presbiterorum defunctus fuerit CCLXIV
Ut si quis cum uxore alterius vivente eo CCXXVII
Ut viginti quattuor biduane similiter cum tribus CCXCVI

Vidue si priusquam continentiam profiteantur nubere CCXV
Viri inter femora fornicans unum annum LXV

Attributions of Canons

A. Councils

Agde XXI, LXXVIII, CLXVI, CCXLIV
African XI, CCXXXV, CCLII, CCLIII
Altheim CCXXVII
Amiens CCCLIX
Ancyra XXXI, XLV, XLVI, XLVII, LXXII, LXXIII, CIII, CLXXXVII, CLXXXVIII
Arles CXVI, CXXVIII, CCXXX, CCLXI
Auxerre (Urbicum) CCLXXXV

Braga XCIX

Carthage CXXXIX, CLXXXI, CCXIII, CCXXXIV, CCXXXVI, CCXLV, CCXLVI, CCXLVII, CCXLVIII, CCLI, CCLXX, CCLXXI
Chalcedon XV, XXXIX, LXXXI, CIV, CCLXXXII
Chalons CCXXII
Constantinople XVI, XVIII

Elvira XXIII, XXX, XXXII, XLI, XCIII
Epao CCCXXXV
Ex decretis sanctorum patrum conciliorum XCIV

Gangra CCLXVI, CCLXVII, CCLXXII, CCLXXIV

Hibernensis Synodus XXII, LI, CXXXIV, CLIV, CLXV, CCLXXXVII, CCLXXVIII

In concilii canonum XXVIII
Iudicium sinodali CCLVI

Laodicea LXXXIX, CCLIX, CCLXXVII
Lerida LXIV, CXLIII

Mainz IV, XX, LXXXIII, LXXXVII, CLI, CCXXIII, CCXLI, CCLXVIII
Meaux LXXXVI, CCXXV

Nantes LXXXVIII
Neocaesarea XC, CCLXXIII
Nicea XIII, LIV, LXXX, CXV, CCXL

Orange CLXXII, CLXXIII, CCLVII, CCLXXVIII, CCLXXIX
Orleans XXV, CXXV, CCXLII, CCL, CCLXII, CCLXIX

Paris CCXVI

Romana Synodus XII, XXIV, XXXIII, LXXXII, CXIX, CXXXIII,CLVI, CLXIV, CCLIV, CCXC, CCLXXXIV
Rouen CCLXIII

Sardica CCLXXXVI
Seligenstadt CCVII

Thionville CCXXXVIII, CCLVIII
Toledo CLVII, CLXXXVI, CLXXXIX, CXV, CCXLIII, CCLXXV
Tribur CCXXIV, CCXXVI, CCLV, CCLXV

Valence CCIX
Verberie (Vermeria) CC, CCI

Zarragosa CLXXVII

B. POPES

Alexander V, CCV, CCCXXII
Anacletus CCXXXI, CCCI, CCCV, CCCXV, CCCXXX
Anicius CCCLXX

Boniface CLIII, CCCX: Ps.-Bonifacius, CCCLXIV

Calixtus CCCXIX,CCCXLIII
Celestine II, CXCVIII, CXCIX, CCCCXXV, CCCXLIV
Clement CCCLVI
Cornelius CCCXXI

Eugenius CCCL, CCCLII
Eutychianus CLXXI
Evaristus CCCXXIX

Fabian CCX, CCXI, CCCLXII, CCCLXXI
Felix IX,CCCXLI

Gelasius CCCLII
Gregory (I) VII, X, XLIV, LXIII, LXVI, LXXXV, XCVIII, CXXIII, CXXVI, CXXVII, CLXII, CXXVII, CL, CLXI, CLXIII,CLXIX, CLXXV, CXCIII, CCXCI, CCCVI, CCCVII, CCCVIII, CCCXIII, CCCXXXII, CCCXLIII, CCCXLVII, CCCXLVIIIX, CCCXLIX, CCCLIIII, CCCLIV, CCCLV, CCCLX, CCCLXV,

CCCLXVI, CCCCLXVII, CCCLXVIII, CCCLXIX, CCCLXXIII, CCCLXXIV, CCCLXXV, CCCLXXVI, CCCLXXVII, CCCLXXVIII
Gregory (II) CCLXXXIX
Gregory (VII) CCVIII with Urban II

Hormisdas XCVII with Eugenius, CCXII, CCXIV, CCXXXIV
Hyginus CCCXXVIII, CCCXXXI, CCCXXXVI

Innocent CCXXI, CCCLXXII

Johannes CLIX, CCCXI
Julius CLII, CCXVIII, CCCIII, CCCXXIV

Leo VI, CV, CVI, CCII, CCCVI, CCCIX, CCCXIV
Liberius CCCLXI
Lucius CCCLIII

Martinus CXVIII, CCCXXXIX

Nicholas CCXXVIII, CCXXIX

Paschal (II) CCCXXVII
Pius CXXXII, CLXVIII, CCCXXXVIII

Sergius CCCXII
Soterius CLXXX, CCCXXXVII
Stephen CCCXVIII
Sylvester XIX, CXIV, CLXXIX, CCCII, CCCXX, CCCXLVI
Symmachus CCCIV
Syricius CIX, CXVII, CCCXLV

Telesphorus CCCXVII, CCCXL

Urban (II) CCIV, CCCXXVII

Vigilius CCCXXXXIII

Zacharius CXX with Deusdedit, CXXI with Deusdedit, CCVI

C. Others

Anonymous I, III, XVII, XXXIV, XXXV, XXXVI, XXXVII, XXXVIII, XLII, LVI, XCVII, CVIII, CX, CXXIV, CXLII,CLV, CLVIII, CLXII, CLXXV, CXCII, CXCIV, CCII, CCIII, CCXXXI, CCXXXII, CCXXXII, CCXXXIII, CCXXXVII, CCXXXIX, CCXLIII, CCLIV, CCLIX, CCLXIV, CCLXXXI, CCXCII, CCXCII, CCXCIII, CCXCIV, CCXCV, CCXCVI, CCXCVII, CCXCVIII, CCXCIX, CCXCIX, CCXCIX, CCC, CCCXVI, CCCXXIII, CCCLVII

Augustine LVIII, XLIX, L, CLXXIV, CLXXVI, CXCVI, CXCVII, CCXXXI, CCCLVIII
Ambrose CLXXVIII, CCXX

Bede Penitential LVII, CLXXXIII, CLXXXIV

Canones apostolorum CXII, CXXII, CCXLIX
Corrector (Burchard) LIX, LX, LXI, LXII, CVIII, CX,CXI, CXXIX, CXXX, CXXXI, CXL
Chrysostom CII, CVII with Theodore and Cummean
Cummean XIV, XLII, XLIII, LV, LVI, LXVIII, LXIX,LXXV, LXXVI, LXXVII, LXXIX, LXXXIV, XCI, XCII, XCV, XCVI, C, CI, CXXXVI, CXXXVII, CLXVII
Cyprian CLXXVIII

Fructuosus CLXXXV

Henry I CCLXXXIII
Hilary CLXXVIII

Isidore CXXXV, CCXVII
Iudicium canonum XXVII, XL, LIII, CXIII, CCLXXX

Jerome LII, CXLIX with Paterius, CCCLVIII
Justinian CCLX

Novellae CCXIX

Penitentiale Romanum XXIX, LVIII, LXV, CXXVIII, CLX, CLXX, CLXXXII, CXC, CCXCIX

Smaragdas VIII

Theodore XXVI, LXVII, LXX, LXXI, LXXIV, CXXIV, CXLI, CXLIV with Cummean, CXLV with Cummean, CXLVI with Cummean, CXLVII with Cummean, CXLVIII with Cummean, CXCI, CXCV, CCLXXVI

Subject Index

abortion/contraception XLVIII, XLIX, L
abstinence CXCIV, CCXX
accusations CCCXV, CCCXVI, CCCXVII, CCCXVIII, CCCXIX, CCCXX, CCCXXI, CCCXXII, CCCXXIII, CCCLXXI
adultery CVII, CXI, CCXXI, CCXXV, CCLVI, CCCXXVIII
alms CCCLXI
altar CCLXVI, CCLXVIII, CCCXXXIV, CCCXXXV
anger CXLIV, CXLV, CXLVI, CXLVII, CXLVIII
arson XXVIII, CLII, CLVIII
auguries *see* divination
authorities CCCLXXII
avarice CCCLVI

baptism CCLXXVI, CCLXXVII, CCLXXVIII, CCLXXXV, CCCXLV, CCCXLVI, CCCXLVIII
beard CCXLVII
beatings XXIII, XXXV, XXXVII, XXXVIII
bestiality LXXIII, LXXIV
bishop XIII, CCCLXXIII, CCCLXXIV

calumny CCXXXVII
canons regular CCVIII
celibacy/chastity, clerical CXIV, CXV, CXVI, CXVII, CXVIII, CXCVIII, CXCIX , CCIV
children LI, LII, CCLXI, CCLXXVI, CCLXXIX, CCCLXVII, CCCLXXV
chrism CCLXXVII, CCLXXVIII, CCLXXIX, CCCXXXV, CCCXLV, CCCXLVI
Christmas CCXLIV
clerical deposition CCLXXV
clerical immunity CCXXXIII, CCXXXVIII
clerics XIV, CCXXXVI, CCXXXIX, CCXLIII, CCXLV, CCXLVI, CCXLVII, CCXLVIII, CCLX
clerics, appointment of CCLXV
clerics, lapsed/degraded CCCLXXXIV, CCCXLIII, CCCLIV
clerics, sons of CCVIII
clerics, wandering CCLXIX, CCLXX
concubines CXII, CXIII, CCCLII
confession V, VII
consecration of church CCCXXVIII, CCCXXIX
Constituta Gregorii pape CCLXXXIX
contempt of church CCLIX
contraception *see* abortion
corporale CCLXVII
councils *see* synods
cousin CCLXXXIX
custom CCCXXXVIII

deaconess CCLXXIX
dead CCCLXV, CCCLXVII

demons XXIV
deposits/loans CCCLVI, CCCLVII, CCCLVIII, CCCLIX
depredation/violation of ecclesiastical/monastic property CLIV, CLV, CLIX, CLX, CCXXXI, CCLIV, CCLVI, CCLX, CCCXXVIII
discipline I
disturbance CCCLXVIII
divination/auguries/magic CLXXXVI, CLXXXVII, CLXXXVIII, CLXXXIX, CXC, CXCI, CXCII
doctrine I
drunkenness CLXXXII, CLXXXIII, CLXXXIV, CLXXXV

Easter CCXLIV
envy CCLII
eucharist, reception CLXXVI, CLXXVII, CLXXVIII, CLXXIX, CLXXX, CLXXXI, CCIII, CCIV, CCXLIV, CCCXXX
eucharist, species CLXVII, CLXVIII, CLXIX, CLXX, CLXXI, CLXXII, CLXXIII, CLXXIV, CLXXV
examination of sins III
executions XXVI

false penance CXCIII
false testimony CXXXVI, CXXXVII, CXXXVIII, CXXXIX, CXL
famine CCCLXI
fasting CCXLII, CCLXXII, CCXC, CCXCIII, CCCXXVI
feasting CCXLV
fighting CCLV
flattery CCXLVIII
foreigners XXIX, CI
fornication LIX, LX, LXI, LXII, LXXVIII, LXXIX, LXXXI, LXXXII, LXXXIII, LXXXIV, LXXXV, LXXXVI, LXXXVII, LXXXVIII, XC, XCIV, XCV, XCVI, XCVII, XCVIII, XCIX, C, CI, CII, CXVIII, CXIX, CXX, CXXII, CXXII, CXCIX, CC, CCI, CCXX, CCXXVII

genuflexion CCXL
godparent/godchild XCV, CXCIX, CCXXIII, CCXXIV, CCXXVIII, CCXXIX, CCXXX, CCLXXXIX, CCCLV
graves CLVII, CCC

hair CCXLVII, CCLXXXIX, CCCLXX
hatred CXLII, CXLIII
haughtiness CCCXLII
homicide XIII, XIV, XV, XVI, XVII, XVIII, XX, XXI, XXII, XXIV, XXVII, XXXII, XXIX, CXXII, CCLV, CCCXXVIII
honor CCCLIII, CCCLXIII
humility CCCXLII

ignorance of canons by priests II
immunity CCLV, CCLVII, CCLVIII, CCLXII, CCLXXXVII
in extremis CXCV, CXCVI, CXCVII, CCII, CCII, CCCXLV
infanticide XL, XLI, XLII, XLIII, XLIV, XLV, XLVI, XLVII
intercourse CVIII
intinction CCIII

Jews XX, CI

kinswoman CCLXXXIX

laughter CCXLVI
laypeople XVII, CXIII, CCXXXVII
Lenten abstinence XCIII

lesbian behavior LXX, LXXI, LXXII
lessons at meals CCXXXV
letters commendatory CCLXX
liberty of monks and monasteries CCCVIII, CCCIX, CCCXI, CCCXIV
litany, major CCXLI
loans *see* deposits
lying CXLIX

magic *see* divination
malice XXXI, XXXII
Mass CCV, CCVI, CCVII, CCXLIII, CCCXXIX, CCCXXX, CCCXXXIII, CCCXXXVII, CCCXL
masturbation *see* pollution
matrimony LXXX, LXXXIX, XCI, CIX, CCXII, CCXIII, CCXIV, CCXVIII, CCXIX, CCXXI, CCXXII, CCXXIII, CCXXIV, CCXXVI, CCXXVII, CCXXVIII, CCXXIX, CCXXX, CCLXXIII, CCLXXIV, CCLXXXIX, CCCLII, CCCLX, CCCLXVI
meals CCLXXI, CCLXXIII
menstruation CI, CCXXXI, CCCLXXVIII
money CCL, CCLI, CCLXXXVI, CCLXXXVIII
monks/monasteries XCI, XCIV, CIX, CXIX, CXXV, CLVI, CXLVI, CLXXXV, CCVIII, CCXLVI, CCLX, CCLXIX, CCLXX, CCLXXXV, CCCV, CCCVII, CCCVIII, CCCIX, CCCX, CCCXI, CCCXII, CCCXIII, CCCXIV, CCCLV, CCCLXXVII
Montecassino CCCXI, CCCXII, CCCXIII, CCCXIV
murder *see* homicide
mutilation LIII, LIV

niece CCLXXXIX
nocturnal emission *see* pollution
Normans CCCXIII
nuns XCI, CIX, CCLXXXIX

oaths *see* vows
offerings CLIII, CCIX, CCX, CCXXXI, CCLXIII
office, divine CCXLIII
olive groves CCLXXXIX
ordination CCCLXXIV, CCCLXXV, CCCLXXVI

pagans XX
penance IV, V, X, XI, XII, CXCIII, CCXCI, CCXCII, CCXCIV, CCXCV, CCXCVI, CCXCVII, CCXCVIII, CCXCIX, CCCXXIV, CCCXXV
penitent IX, XIX
pentecost CCXLIV
perjury CXXII, CXXIII, CXXIV, CXXVI, CXXVII, CXXVIII, CXXIX, CXXX, CXXXI, CXXXII, CXXXIII, CXXXIV, CXXXV
persecution CCCXLIII
pestilence CCCLXI
pimping CVIII
pollution/nocturnal emission/ masturbation LV, LVI, LVII, LVIII, LXXV, LXXVI, LXXVII
possessions of churches CCLXXXI, CCLXXXII, CCCLI
presbyteress CCLXXXIX
primacy of the Roman Church CCCI, CCCII, CCCIII, CCCIV
privileges, authority of CCCV, CCCVI, CCCVII
Proprie auctoritates apostolice sedis CCXCIX

prostitute CXXI

quatember days CCCXXVI

raptus CIII, CIV, CV, CVI, CCXVII, CCLXII, CCLXXXIX
reconciliation CCCLXII
restoration of churches CCCXXXI, CCCXXXII, CCCXXXIII
rogation days CCXLII

sacrilege CL, CLI, CCXXXI
scurrility CCXLVI
sedition CCLIII
servants XXI, XXII, XXIII, XXXIV, C
shipwreck CCLXXXIII, CCCXXVII
sins I, VIII, XI
sister-in-law CCLXXXIX
slander CXLI
sodomy LXIII, LXIV, LXV, LXVI, LXVII, LXVIII, LXIX
spectacle CCCXXXIX
stepmother CCLXXXIX
subdeacon CCIV
Sunday CI, CLXXIX, CCXL, CCLXXX, CCCXLIX, CCCL
surety CCXXXIV
synods/councils CCCXLI, CCCLXIV

theft XXV, CXXII, CLX, CLXI, CLXII, CLXIII, CLXIV, CLXV, CLXVI, CCXXXI, CCLXXXVII, CCLXXXVIII
tithes CCXI, CCXXXII
tonsure CCCLXX
traitor XXXIII, CCXLVIII

usurpation of church CCLXIV
usury CCXLIX, CCL, CCLIII

violation of ecclesiastical/monastic property *see* depredation...
virgin CCLXXXIX
virgines subintroductae CXV
virginity XCII
vows/oaths CXXV, CCXXXIII, CCCLXXVII

widow CCXV, CCXVI, CCLXXXIX
wine CCCXLV
wood of church CCCXXXVI